100 things to learn before you're 10

By
Gail Hugman
Cert. Ed., T. Dip. M

Published by
The Endless Bookcase Ltd.
71 Castle Road, St Albans, Hertfordshire,
England, UK, AL1 5DQ.

www.theendlessbookcase.com

Printed in the United Kingdom
Also available in multiple e-book formats.
First Printing, 2017

Copyright © 2017 Gail Hugman
All rights reserved.

ISBN: 978-1-908941-98-5

Aliyah Aden Adam Ana Juan Pablo Anna Amy Aoife Asha Astrid

Kallista Melissa Celia Chantel Charlene Charlotte Henry Chloe Joanna

David Clare Claire Danielle Dominique Elise Ella Ben Ella Rose James

Ella Elaine Emily Emilie Emma Ema Fleur Jack Florence Georgina Grace

Greta Joe Hannah   Hazel Holly Izzy

Jade Jackie   J a s m i n e

J e m i m a   This book is   Jennie Jo
                              dedicated to the children
Julia Emilio   of the world; especially those   Julia Julie
                               who have inspired and
J u l i e t   motivated this work.   Vinnie Kara

K i r s t y   Whatever the culture may tell   K a t h e r i n e
                              you, always believe in yourself
Kate Kelly   and forever strive to be the   Katy   Kate
                              best you can be; it makes
Laura Laura Lara   a difference.   Leanne Leah Lily

Lisa Lisa Lizzy Louise   Lulu Lucy Tallulah Myra

Mona Lina Rebecca Rihanna Sadie Samantha Sara Sarah Sian Sofia

Sophia Stephanie Suzanne Tina Tracy Tula Una Isabel Zara Zoe Tyler

Robert Michael Tej Jai Percy Celeste Aman Henry William Charles

Callum Harry Harry Harrison Luke Matthew Jimmy Sam Eliot Arthur

Sid James Jack Cassius Cedric Abdullah Daniel Danny Darren Darren

Robbie Douglas Alastair Jonathan Scott Leo Luke Luis Oliver

Oscar Ruben Toby Michael Joshua Terry Theo Thomas Tom

With love, thanks and appreciation for listening, believing, supporting, encouraging and for keeping the inspiration alive while this book was being written …oh, and for the practical business of producing it.

Thank you all so much!!

Tanya
Neil & Mary
Neil
Carl
Morgana
Monica
Nick
Penny
Sarah
Jerry
and parents everywhere….

About the author

Gail started teaching in 1974. It was pre-National Curriculum. Teachers were left very much to their own initiative and devices in the Social Priority Area school where her teaching began in Haringey.

Gail's experience includes whole class teaching, covering the full primary age range. In addition to this, she ran a unit for disruptive pupils in Islington for three years; became a Home Tutor for children who had been excluded from school in Haringey and has worked with children with complex special needs. She has been praised by OFSTED on several occasions for her resourcefulness, creative teaching and her ability to bring out the best in even the most challenging of children. She held various senior management roles during her 30 years in schools.

Her experience includes teaching for a year in the USA and attending training in a school in Israel, where they have a different and interesting approach to education based in human development. She was also invited to observe and discuss educational issues in schools in South Africa and Mauritius. (From this she reports that playgrounds sound the same wherever you are in the world!)

In 2005, Gail established Lessons Alive as a teaching and development service. Her experience in schools, coupled with her private work with parents and their children in their homes, has given her a unique perspective on the real issues faced by young learners and their parents.

Lessons Alive creates bespoke lessons to help address the individual child's specific needs so that they can establish a firm foundation for learning and living; helping to motivate, inspire and empower the child to take responsibility and engage in a meaningful and purposeful way in their education and development.

Birth to puberty is the foundation building phase of life and Gail believes it is crucial that parents, teachers and children themselves appreciate the processes involved during this period. Using her research, experience and observation she creates new and insightful talks and workshops for parents and teachers to boost their confidence and help them do the best job they can for each child.

100 things to learn before you're 10

Contents

Introduction 1
First things first 7
About Motivation - a closer look at the situation 9
Core Alignment and Attitude 11
Lesson 1: The Two Lives 15
Poem: Alone we cannot change the world 18
Lesson 2: Your brain is meant to work for you! 19

    It begins this way: 20

    An example of how to train your brain to work for you: Learning Times Tables 31

    Dazzle 32

Lesson 3: Start Here 37
Poem: We see the trees and flowers 45
Lesson 4: Time 47

    More ways to help your child appreciate 'a minute' and learn more about themselves and what they are capable of: 49

    Using Time 50

    When children need to speed up their work rate: 57

Lesson 5: Listening 61

    Teaching your child to listen 62

    What children need to know about listening - reference that is helpful for the brain and how to develop the skill 63

    Activities for teaching Listening to your child 65

        The Sound Maker Hunt 66

        Activity: The Jumpasound 67

Activity: The Back to Back Book 68

　　Activity: The Outside Sounds - investigations…........................ 69

Lesson 6: THE BUBBLE STRATEGY 71

　　Sixteen questions to ask yourself and reflect on if your child
　　does not listen: 73

**Lesson 7: A little bit about the learning process... older
children (7+) love to know! 75**

Lesson 8: Concentration 79

　　Defining Concentration for your child (reference) 80

　　Daily starter: to develop and strengthen concentration skills: 81

Lesson 9: Feelings 85

　　Helping children manage feelings - first they need reference: 86

　　How to talk to children about negative feelings and how to
　　manage them. 86

　　Negative feelings that make a human being feel 'bad': 87

　　When you meet negativity in your child, the following responses
　　may be helpful in realigning your child to the best of themselves: .. 90

　　Common negative feelings in children that can trigger a
　　challenging reaction: 90

Poem: The oldest in his family 93

**Lesson 10: Boundaries, Consequences and Taking
Responsibility 95**

　　The Two Sets of Rules we inherited at birth: 95

　　　Natural - inflexible, fixed, core natural boundaries 95

　　　Man made - flexible, not fixed 96

　　Managing a Tantrum 98

Poem: Setting Boundaries 101

Lesson 11: Comprehension 103

Lesson 12: What Children need to know about School 107

Lesson 13: Organisation and Planning 111

    Planning 115

    Reference to give an appreciation of time - the foundation for planning 116

    Setting Targets with your child 121

    Important Points to get across to your child about the Advantages of Planning and why they need to learn to do it: 121

    Planning for Success - when you are in an exam year 122

Lesson 14: Homework 125

    For homework to be successful and meaningful your child needs: 127

    Here's a simple way to remember what you need for HOMEWORK: 128

    Homework Kit Checklist 135

    Cooling down your brain! 137

Lesson 15: A Way to Think about Skills, Children and Development 139

Poem: The culture that we live in 146

Lesson 16: What children need to know about habits 149

Poem: Habit 155

50 Most Loved, Most Used, Most Useful Books for Children from 4 -12 years old selected from the Teacher's Personal Collection.... 157

Top 21 Most Loved and used Games and Activities for Teaching Skills to primary aged children 161
    ACTIVITIES: no or low cost resources 161
    GAMES that can be purchased. 163
100 things to learn before you're 10 169

Introduction

> It was September 2001 and the first day of term. The head teacher had forgotten that a student teacher would be coming to do observation and at the last minute, asked if he could observe my Year 6 class for the morning. I agreed and the bell announced the start of the school day. As the children poured into the classroom, pushing and shoving each other, jostling for what they considered the 'best seats' (near the back), I took a deep breath to call them to order, caught sight of the student teacher in the corner and stopped. I waited - doing my own observation while recalling my experience as a newly qualified teacher almost 30 years earlier when two, silent lines of children were led in from the playground to the classroom. The comparison was stark. It isn't that 1974 was 'right' and 2001 was 'wrong'; the difference caused me to start questioning what children really need in the preparation, foundation and bedrock on which they would build their lives. It made me question why so many children can behave in such an unruly way, or can 'switch off' in school (and at home); why so many children underperform or underachieve; what really causes a lack of confidence; low self-esteem or bullying? I waited 15 minutes that morning for the children to settle down and you can read what happened next in the poem called Setting Boundaries later in this book

Not long after this, I happened to be accompanying a group of children on a visit to a science event and we travelled in a neighbouring school's minibus. The driver was their young, dynamic Year 6 teacher, who was on the 'fast track to headship' scheme. On the return journey, I asked him what bothered him most in teaching. His answer was almost immediate: 'Motivation.' He went on to say that he could 'get the children to do what they needed to do', but he couldn't 'get them to *want* to do it'. I realised that if we were going to make any real difference, we need to focus on this '*getting them to want to do it*' and dig deep to get to the underlying causes of poor motivation, poor behaviour, negative attitudes and fixed mindsets.

I stopped teaching in school the next year and began presenting talks to local parents about motivating children. The talks were well attended and well received but there would always be parents waiting at the end who would thank me very much for the talk and end with, 'but will *you* come and talk to my child' and it became clear that there is often a gap between what children need and what many parents feel confident to deliver. This book has been written to help those parents bridge that gap. Here are some of the questions raised by parents themselves, when asked what they were looking for:

- To learn more about and get the best/most out of my children in terms of learning and motivation.

- To get them engaged.

- Ways to connect with my child that can help her grow emotionally and reduce anxiety.

- Ways to think about helping my children as they grow (and learn).

- To understand my child's approach to learning.

- How to be patient.

- My child to do what he's told without a war.

- A calmer, smoother running household.

- A child that is keen to learn.

- To support my 4 year old when he starts school in September.

- To help my children feel better and enjoy their learning as well as self-motivation and self-discipline.

- To motivate and fire him up so that he can understand or 'see' his own potential and the possibilities open to him and not be afraid to reach out for them.

- To understand different behaviours to learning and how to motivate my children through school.

- Everyone to believe in themselves.

- Tips on how to control their moods without getting angry with them.

- To know how to understand my seven year old child better.

- To motivate my child to want to do their homework ...and to check their homework...

- To be able to teach my children to be respectful in and outside of the home.

- My child to concentrate! How to speak/ask questions with a sensible answer. Keeping them motivated. Getting a response.

These questions are typical of many asked by parents who are juggling the demands of modern life and work, while they are raising their children. They may often feel their children 'could do better' and become very concerned if the child's school highlights this in a report, but many parents aren't so confident with changing children's attitudes or what to teach or how to really motivate and encourage them, especially if the children have 'switched off' and no longer respond to what their parents say.

This book is going to help by addressing these issues and questions. It's going to look at the reasons why so many children underperform at school and what can be done about aligning them at core, so that they stay connected to the positive influences that are in them at birth. It puts forward tried and tested lessons, tools and strategies that have been developed during forty years of teaching experience and which have been repeatedly proven effective with children. It takes a step back and offers a fresh pair of eyes to look at childhood; its' purpose and human development.

It is during the first 12 years after birth that each life develops the framework for its future. It is a critical time in our lives because everything that happens during the period from birth to puberty has an affect on the foundation of that life. We know, for example, that if the child's hearing or vision is impaired in some way, it can have a direct affect on the development of their brain and learning. If they experience a major trauma, such as bereavement or divorce, it will interrupt their natural line of development and process and the consequences can more often than not, ricochet throughout their childhood and into adult life, even leading the individual into therapy if the effects are interfering in their ability to make progress or feel fulfilled.

One of the reasons for this seems to be that half our education is missing. In general, we tell children to 'listen' without explaining what that really means; we say they need to 'concentrate' without telling them how, in any way that is meaningful to them; so it is not what we say or teach that leaves a child's development vulnerable to confusion. It is more often what we *don't* say or do that leaves the way wide open to misunderstanding and misalignment. In general, ignorance about the brain and human development; poor reference; misinterpreting children's behaviour and not understanding what children *really* want, all contribute to their underperformance and underachievement.

Children frequently feel as though they have to 'wait to grow up before they can 'do' anything'. Lack of reference makes them unable to express their needs articulately and what they meet, or what they are asked to do, can feel like an imposition; a control and constriction, because in their eyes it can appear to conflict with their natural line of development (what they *feel* like doing), which is where they are based. This is one of the reasons they may switch off; rebel; lack motivation or develop 'attitude'. What children really want and *need* at core is meaningful development. It is what human beings are designed for. The internal drives born in each of us are designed to be acted upon and, as with all things in nature, will do everything to find a way to be expressed and to grow. When the environment is not supportive; development is temporarily arrested. To remain, or reconnect, to inspiration and motivation, children need help to make the connections between personal growth and life as they live it coupled with the education they receive at school. Although it would be ideal if this was explicitly included in the curriculum and taught in school, the reality is that in a class of 30 children, each child can receive *just 10 minutes per day* of individual attention from their teacher and *only if all other teaching activities and duties are suspended!*

With the best will in the world, we all know this is simply not enough time to teach a child what they need to know about themselves; about the world; the culture; and about their purpose so that they can be the best that *they* can be, in attitude, motivation, independence, presentation, organisation, listening and concentration skills. Many naturally bright children develop low self-esteem, lack of confidence, frustration, boredom, poor presentation, underperformance; underachievement and/or cheekiness as a result of disconnection or distance from the core of themselves.

This is where parents can definitely help and this book aims to pass on the foundation building development knowledge and tools that have been shown to work. Every child can benefit from this work, *either to resolve an issue or to pre-empt difficulties that may arise*, because it puts things in perspective and gives them a sense of purpose and direction. They feel confirmed and empowered and have been shown to become happier, better motivated and independent as a result. This in turn has raised levels of achievement and exam scores. Although it is preferable that these lessons are taught by the time a child reaches puberty, they are extremely helpful for the alignment of teenagers who have not had them and who may need help to see 'the bigger picture' and to understand the processes they are experiencing so they, too, can feel more motivated and in control of their own future.

It really doesn't matter what nationality you are; the one thing *everyone* has in common - *all* children - *all* adults - wherever we are in the world, whatever language we speak, whatever faith or lifestyle we adhere to, is that we are all **human at core**. This does not simply mean a physical sameness (although, whatever colour our skin or shape our features, our basic shape remains the same), but that we were all designed *to work the same way*. There is a human blueprint we can recognise in all babies at birth.

This book is about preserving and developing the human core in your child by giving them what they need at core and helping them to make the connections they need during their formation. The lessons draw on the knowledge of **what works** and **what doesn't work**. It is a dip-in-and-out book, not a sit down, start-at-the-beginning-and-keep-going riveting read, book. It is a book to be kept handy for when parents need it.

'*100 Things to Learn before you're 10*' is filled with a lot of common sense which is coupled with insights, reasons and reinforcing things-that-need-to-be-said that deep down everyone 'knows', but that are all too often assumed, left to chance or overlooked so *very few people think to teach them!* There are examples and stories to illustrate how the lessons can be used. The information covers the missing links, the bits the core of each child **needs to understand** so that they engage with the process of living and don't lose sight of its sense of purpose.

First things first

There is an intuitive sense in all of us, whether we recognise it or not, that tells us 'the world is not right'. We tell the children to 'be kind', to 'be polite', 'work hard', 'share' and 'not fight' but we live in a culture which seems to be relentlessly growing in conflict; anger and worse. Raising children to do what we instinctively know to be 'right' in this quagmire of contradictory evidence is stressful at best; often downright challenging and heartbreaking at worst.

If the world is to improve 'for our children', then we need to help them by teaching them two things.

1. What they need to know to **develop** the best of themselves.

2. What they need to know to **recognise** and **manage** the worst.

We all make mistakes. We may not be perfect. We don't need to wallow in it!

Nor can we closet ourselves away, focus solely on 'the perfect development' - if there even is such a thing - and pretend the 21st century does not exist, it does; and although there are those who do try to avoid it, it is simply not practical for most of us.

What these 100 things will help you do is find the way to preserve the integrity of the human core in your children and how to **use the 21st** century to help you do that.

There are hundreds of additional, obvious, practical things a child needs to learn before they are 10 such as: how to walk and dress themselves, how to wash and brush their teeth etc. These were never meant to be included in this book because they are generally covered very well elsewhere and not difficult to find. The purpose of this book is to **highlight where the gaps appear** and **deliver what is needed to fill them.**

100 things to learn before you're 10

The focus of this world - particularly in western cultures - is on how things look rather than on how things actually are in themselves. We say 'good morning' when it is raining; we tell children 'tests don't matter' and then get stressed about the levels they achieve. For the children it can be bewildering and confusing to work out what really *does* matter and who is 'telling the truth'; this book aims to help you explain it to them.

> N.B. Very important note: The 100 things are written the way that they have been most effective in aligning and strengthening children. You are, of course, welcome to adapt them to your own child's needs but if you do, please be careful you do not introduce bias or persuasion or you may lose the essence of what is being taught. The wording is specific. It carries the concept and the meaning and will be understood by children of all ages.

About Motivation - a closer look at the situation

At the time of writing - June 1st 2016 - the world population was:

7,426,510,212

that's seven billion, four hundred and twenty six million, five hundred and ten thousand, two hundred and twelve...

By the time you read this, it will be significantly more.

This may not strike you as being of any real consequence while we are thinking about the motivation of children. However, the year the author was born, the world population was:

2,665,865,392

that's two billion, six hundred and sixty five million, eight hundred and sixty five thousand, three hundred and ninety two....

This means that in less than one lifetime, the world population has practically trebled. So, what does this have to do with child motivation and in particular your child's motivation?

- There is a distinct increase in pressure - if we treble the number of people in the room, we will feel it

- There is an increase in competition - locally, we see this with school places, travel, employment, the health service...

- Levels of pollution have dramatically increased affecting health and well being

- The growth of the 'throw away' culture has seen a weakening in values and quality

- 'Instant' everything has influenced attitudes towards work and self

- Through technology, we are forced to process more information in a day than ever before

The changes in education try to keep pace with the needs of the society we live in, but they don't really have the time, space nor expertise to keep pace with our human development needs as well which is where the children need most help if they are to be independent and confident in the world they now inhabit.

Core Alignment and Attitude

The bright, chatty 7 year old West Indian girl wanted to show off her younger brother who had just started in the nursery of her school. All the children were being seated in the school hall for an assembly. As she pointed him out, she said, 'there he is, next to the boy in the blue jumper and behind the girl with the red bow'....no one could have mistaken her brother; he was the only child of colour in the row but at that point in time, the colour of his skin was not an issue. After an absence of three years, the teacher revisited the school and asked about the bright, little West Indian girl and her family. There had been a change. The girl had become aggressive, looked angry and was underachieving. Apparently, the family had become victims of racism and regularly received abuse and violence around their home. It was a very unhappy situation.

Judgement; criticism; racism; hate and the notion of failure...these are some of the very meaty issues that affect all human beings. None of these destructive forces are present in a human life at birth and yet they continue to thrive in the culture we inhabit and insidiously inveigle each life despite parents best efforts to avoid them. Where is the evidence that 'play nicely' works as either a refinement or a deterrent in your foundation?

The one thing that has remained constant throughout the years, is what a child *is* and how they work, grow and develop. Today's child has the same body, brain, senses and so on as well as the same core development needs that you had at their age, but the culture demands that they process more and at a faster speed than you did at their age. At times, this can result in your child being overwhelmed by negative influences before they have the tools to identify and manage them. This certainly affects their behaviour and motivation.

Children are naturally open; sensitive; perceptive; creative; intelligent; caring; warm and trusting. They come with their own 'agenda' which is to belong and to develop. They need to develop skills, gather experience, form character and contribute their unique talent into the world. However, these very much finer traits and motives are often thwarted and eroded during the process of childhood - by competition; criticism; judgement; racism; ignorance; divorce; adoption; bereavement and the many major disruptions from the world that can happen *during our formation*. The consequences of this are far-reaching because each child's unique talent may never develop to reach the world in the way it was designed to, resulting in a life unfulfilled, disappointed and frustrated - vulnerable to the development of negative attitudes, blaming everyone and everything else, which can then superimpose itself on the core.

The following lesson of the Two Lives gives children the opportunity to put things into perspective. It is a tool which gives you the language to help a child to realign after major disruptions in their life because it gives their brain somewhere to use or place their experience and a way to understand the feelings that they have from it. This has huge implications for children's mental health and behaviour. Any time a child is underperforming; underachieving; depressed; confused or aggressive you will undoubtedly find it is a *perfectly natural reaction* from their core, feeling threatened by a world experience or environment that they haven't got the reference to explain to themselves, never mind to you. The question, 'Why did you do that?' is met by silence. We inherited this culture. It is ours to change by developing the finer aspect of the core and refining the negative as we go. The best way to protect your child is to educate them and give them the reference and tools they need to be independent.

The Two Lives is recommended as a starting point for the alignment, empowerment and confidence of all children. The aspect you want to highlight may change according to the age of the child and the discussion you want to have with them.

You will also find it is a lesson to return to at different stages; to examine closely what is happening on 'the line of life' at each stage and why the child may be feeling what they are feeling and how to move forward. It will help your child talk about and understand the world they are in and give them a sense of direction, purpose and security because *they are naturally based in the core*, called here the 'Natural Life'.

It begins by separating the Two Lives of 'Natural' and 'World', which the children intuitively feel but need help to realise and get into perspective.

It can help de-personalise the lesson and focus the brain if you sit next to your child at a table or on the sofa with some paper and a pencil to draw the diagrams shown as you speak to them. You don't need to be an artist to do this! Going through the thinking process at a speed your child's brain can absorb is what is important, sketching it as you go helps to keep their brain focused on the process and gives them enough time to reflect, understand and ask any questions they may have without feeling pressured.

100 things to learn before you're 10

Lesson 1:
The Two Lives

Draw a line and say: 'If this is the line of life, then between here *(point to 0)* and here *(point to 100)*, you have a job to do. Have you got any idea what that might be? *(Pause, listen to their answers) then say:* 'Between here 0 and here 100, you have to live a life (it might agree with what they said!) and write it above the diagram.

Live a life

0..100

While their brain absorbs this piece of information, add the following ages to the line:

Live a life

0.....10.....20.....30.....40.....50.....60.....70.....80.....90......100

Carry on by explaining:

'The moment you are born, it is as if you are given not one, but Two Lives.

The first we will call your **Natural Life'**

Write on diagram:

Live a life

Natural life

0......10......20......30......40......50......60......70......80......90.....100

'The other we will call your **World Life**'

Write on diagram:

Live a life

Natural life

0......10......20......30......40......50......60......70......80......90.....100

World Life

Start to explain the Two Lives in the following way:

The **Natural Life** is completely automatic and the same for every person, whoever they are and wherever they are in the world. We cannot live without this life. We know that we begin as a child; develop to be a teenager; move into being a young adult, mature adult and senior.'

(You can point at the various stages as you talk about them - child, teenager and so on)...

'As long as you eat, sleep, receive impressions, exercise and keep out of danger, your **Natural Life** will happen without you having to think about it. We grow to adulthood whether we like it or not. The other life, your **World Life**, is not automatic and is different for every person, depending on where you are on the planet; the culture you are born into and the time in history. When we arrive our parents/carers give us a name, teach us to walk, talk, the names of everything and what belongs to us. They teach us about where we live and how to dress ourselves, wash, feed, take care of ourselves and a whole lot more, mostly local, information. They teach us right from wrong and give us an idea of what is expected of us at home and in the world, which can be different in each family.'

'These two lives run alongside and influence each other for our entire lives, but there are some important things you need to know.'

'The **World Life** is meant to give you the experience, tools and opportunities you need to develop and grow your **Natural Life**.'

'**You are not meant to change yourself to be something else to fit into the world**, but it is possible to make this mistake because the culture can sometimes give us that impression and that can make people feel very fed up, because then their **Natural Life** doesn't always feel good enough, or get a chance to shine and develop and they can feel 'stuck'.'

A simple version of **The Two Lives** can be told to children as young as 5 years old.

It is a lesson that can be adapted to be effective all the way up to school leaving age. It is especially valuable for teenagers who are going through puberty and trying to establish their identity at the same time as they are approaching school leaving age or important exams. It helps enormously to describe the processes that are occurring in the Natural Life at this time and the reason why they feel 'all at sea'.

The lesson of **The Two Lives** gives the bigger picture in an unbiased, matter of fact, way. It can be used to discuss learning approaches, personal targets and goals. It is a very valuable lesson to pass on to your children and then to your grandchildren, to prevent them being inadvertently caught up in the whirlwind of the 21st century, which can distract so easily from what is of real importance in life.

Poem:
Alone we cannot change the world

Alone we cannot change the world
The problems are too great
But we can change ourselves inside
Perhaps it's not too late

To rise above all judgement
All criticism and more
It's not an easy thing to do
When reaching for the core

Life is a glittering promise
We're only given once
And if we do not use it
There is no other chance

So look to your own talents
They're yours alone to grow
And when you find the truth of you
The evidence will show

This, the children should receive
They're born into the real
But with deception all around
Confusion's what they feel

Without this education
What future here on earth?
The potential of magnificence
Awaits us from our birth

Lesson 2:
Your brain is meant to work for you!

> A very clever ten year old boy just couldn't see the point of homework. He felt it was a pointless exercise and because of this he would get it 'over and done with', but with a certain degree of resentment and never with any real pride.

Many children feel like this and this brain lesson helps to explain *why* they feel like they feel; why it is not personal; how to get more motivated and in control of it so that homework - and many other things - can become a development tool rather than a chore.

To help your child to get the full benefit of this lesson; it is best to sit beside them with a notepad and pencil and prepare to illustrate what you say as you go. The drawing itself is not that important and can be as simple as you like; the process of sketching as you go through it, means you give their brain something to focus on and reveal the information gradually at a speed the child can easily process and understand, which makes it more effective.

'Your brain is meant to work for you', soon established itself as a core lesson that is definitely of benefit to all children for explaining attitude, self control, purpose, concentration and organisation. This is one of the most valuable tools to empower your child.

It begins this way:

'You may not know, but **your brain is meant to work for you!** It is partly programmed when you are born. We can move, make noise, learn and grow.

If we could look down on the top of your head and see your brain inside, it would look a little like this:'

Draw a circle on a piece of paper

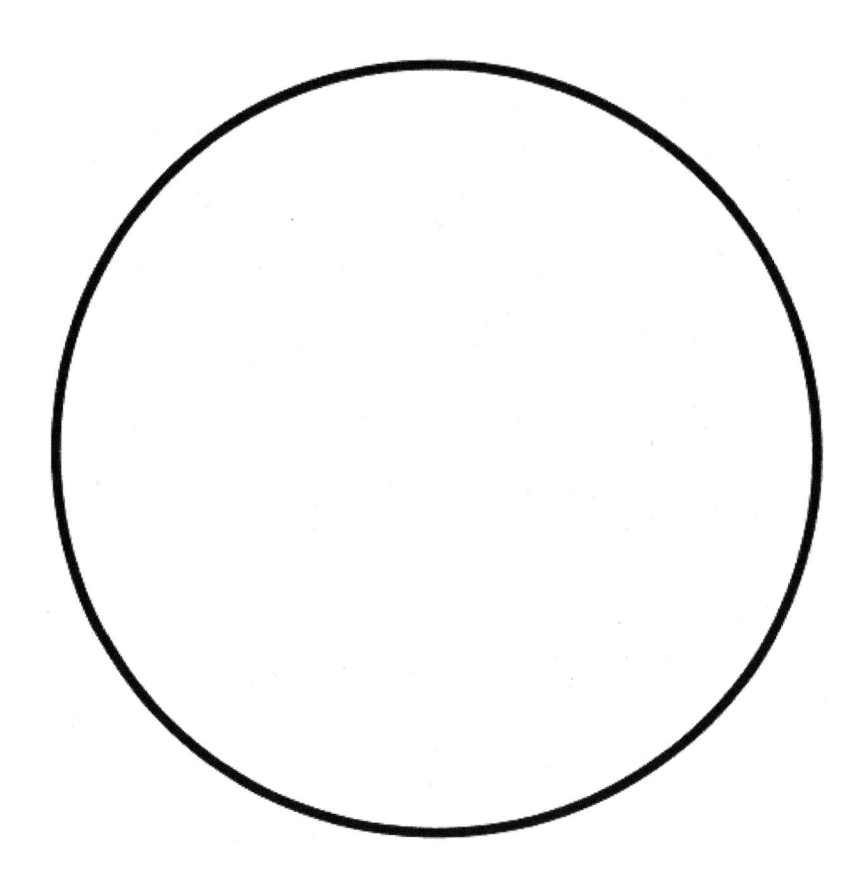

100 things to learn before you're 10

Continue, telling your child: 'It has three main parts, like this.'

Add a semicircle and line to the circle as follows:

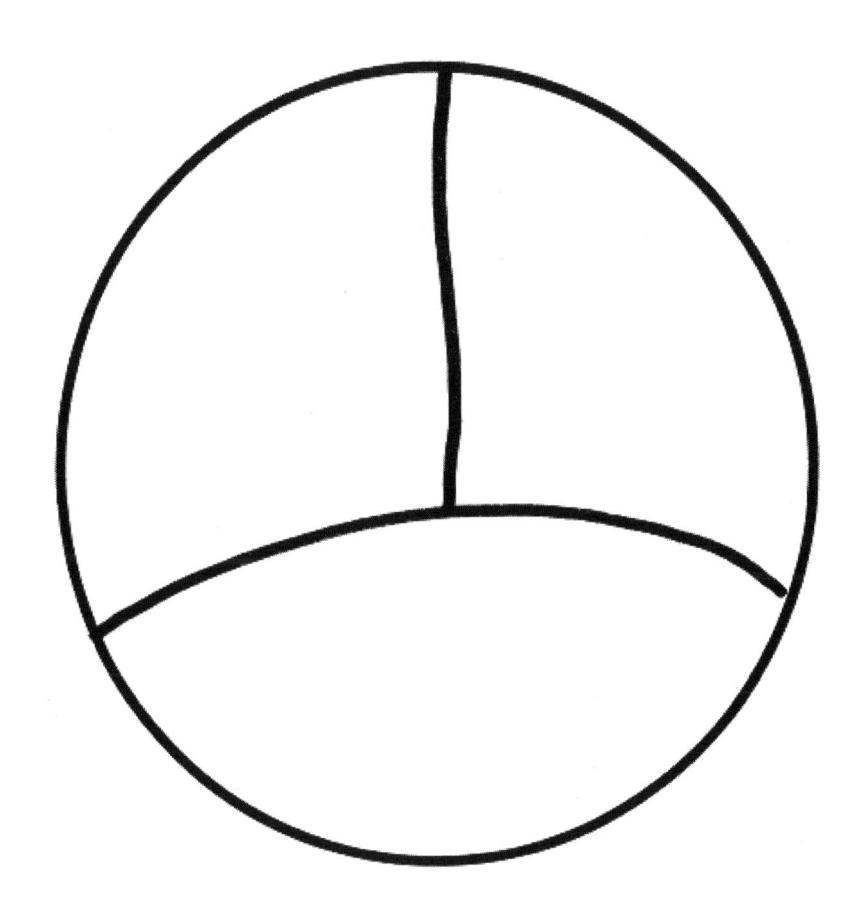

21

100 things to learn before you're 10

'There are two goggly eyes at the front, looking out…..*(draw)* and ears either side', *(draw on the side of the head)*

100 things to learn before you're 10

Explain:

'You don't need to remember the names of these three sections but they are:

Conscious', *(write the word in the front section)* and say: 'this is where we are when we are awake.'

100 things to learn before you're 10

'This bit here'…*(pointing to back left)* 'is called **Semi-conscious.** This is where we do all our thinking and we sort of have it 'talking' quietly in the background most of the time.'

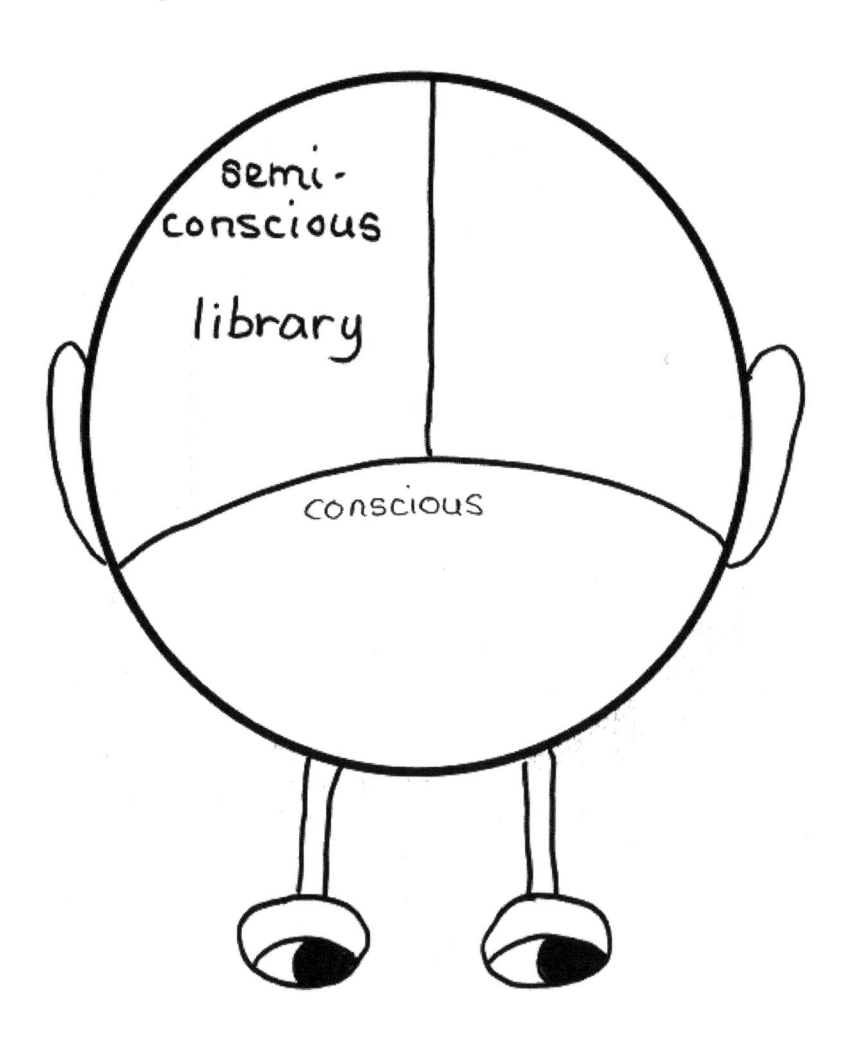

semi-conscious
library

conscious

100 things to learn before you're 10

'And finally, this bit here is the **Unconscious.** This is where we go when we're asleep. It is the part that takes charge of all the automatic things like making our body work and making us better when we are ill or out of sorts.'

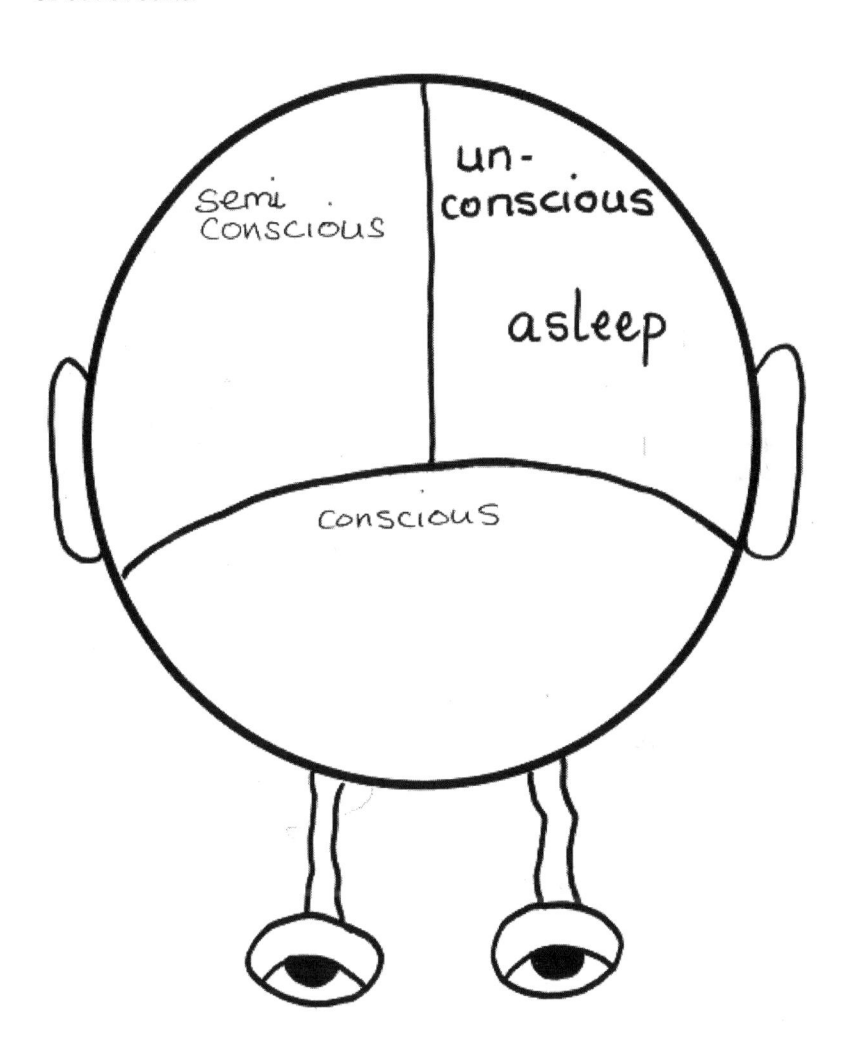

100 things to learn before you're 10

'Now, it's as if there is a little helper in each of these parts and in Conscious, where we are when we're awake *(draw small stick figure helper in C)*, his job is to find out everything new and show it to you or bring it to your attention. It sometimes helps to give him a name, I call mine Rummage!'

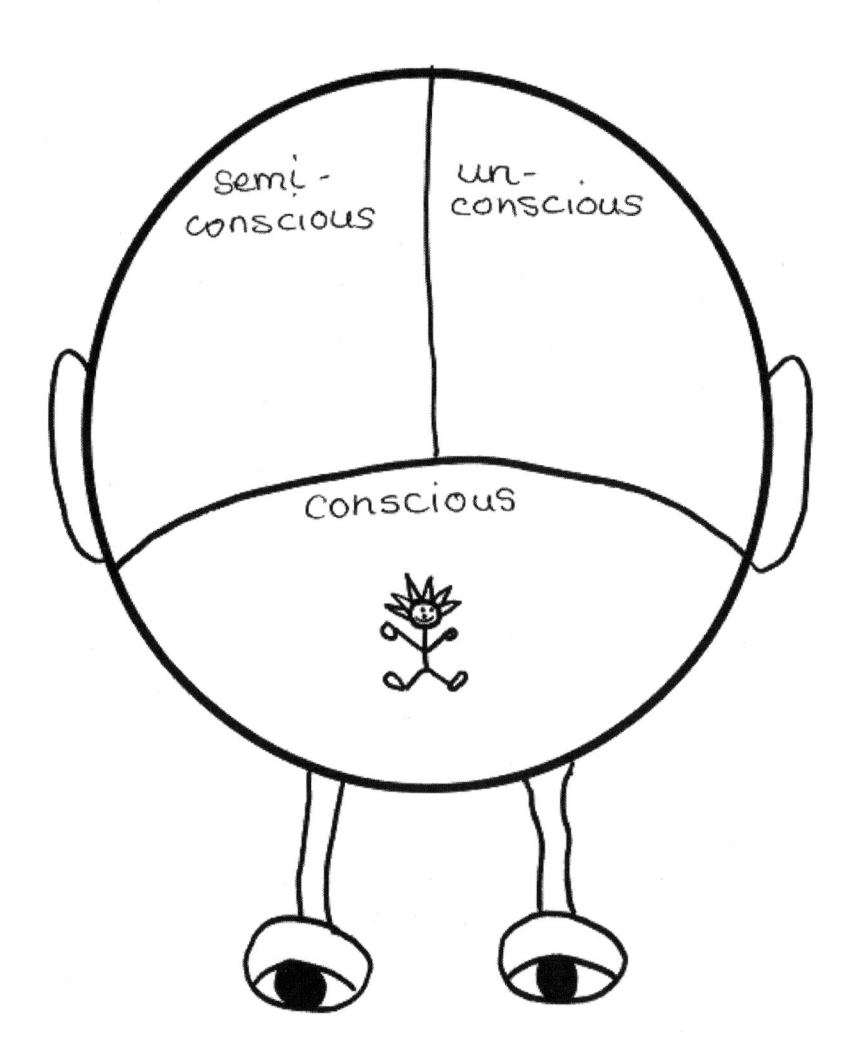

100 things to learn before you're 10

(You can have some fun going through a thesaurus coming up with names for this little helper. Everyone can choose their own, or as a family you can agree on one name that all of you will use)

'Rummage *(or whomever you choose)*, loves colour, noise, excitement and anything moving. Loves dancing, making a spectacle of *your*self, laughing and being mischievous. Likely to love chocolate, staying up late, computer games...you must have got the picture by now - New! New! New! Flash! Exciting! BUT: He has no idea what is good for you and what is not good for you, which is why it's a really good job you've got parents and teachers to help you...

He does **not** like doing things more than once, thinks it's really boring, and so it's not unusual that he just *hates* homework and sometimes even calls on his friend, Whine, to come and complain about it! On the whole though, if he is well managed, he's brilliant and really, really helpful. For example: if you decide that you would like a blue hat with bright red and purple pompoms, he will look in every shop, everywhere you go and he will keep looking, pointing out all the hats with pompoms until you either find the one you're looking for, or you decide to stop looking... (and you do have to tell him to stop or he just goes on looking - because he really wants to help you and he won't know you've changed your mind unless you tell him (that's somewhere else)!!

He can also be a real whizz when it comes to revision, again, properly managed and given direction by you, but more about that later.

Two other things you need to know about Rummage: he doesn't remember anything for very long: so for example if I tell you a number like 87954632 and ask you to remember it, you might be able to say it back to me straight away (can you?)....but it is unlikely you will be able to say it back in two hours time! This is why we have to take control of our learning and when there is something important to learn, from teachers or parents, we have to do things to let Rummage know that it is important and that we want to keep it. He will then pass it through to the Semi Conscious who puts it away in the library for 'Future Reference'.'

100 things to learn before you're 10

Point to the Semi-Conscious in the diagram and draw another little figure:

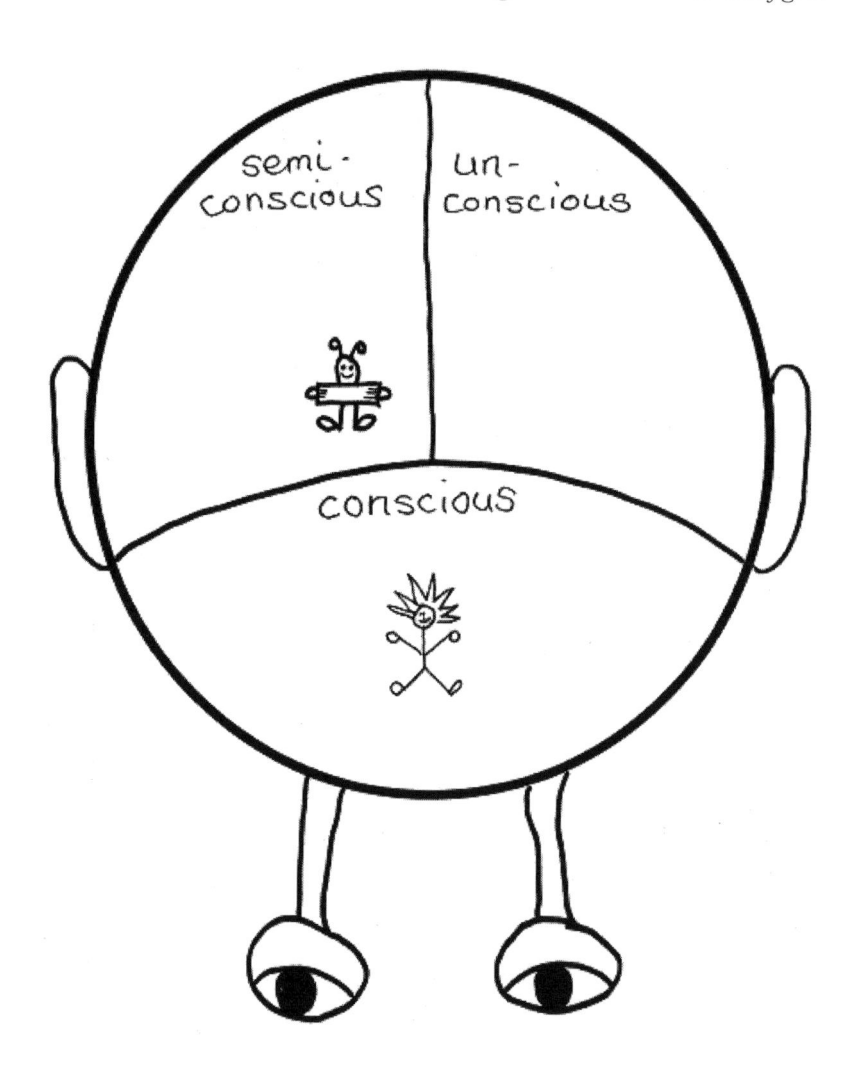

'There is another little helper in here who sits reading the newspaper all day until there is something to find or something to put away. He has a name too and I call him, Stock. What are you going to name yours?

The **Semi-conscious** is a bit like a main library with a little ideas factory inside and the more organised and tidy we are, in our things and in our learning, the more organised and tidy Stock will be (he copies us) and the quicker he can find things when we want them - like when we have exams, for instance!

Everything you have learned is stored in here, so if you know your 3x table it might be in a cupboard or on a shelf back here *(point to somewhere on diagram!)*.

Some things get put away in here because we deliberately put them here, (like when we practise times tables or study something), but some things get put away in the library because they are especially special; like very happy things to remember or sometimes especially sad things that we want to remember to learn from or to remind us of something or someone.

All of our experience is put at the back in these departments here *(point to Semi conscious and Unconscious)* even though we often cannot remember all of it, but we need to keep it to help with comprehension (and probably other stuff when we're older, but we don't need to worry about that, now).

At the moment you are born, your Unconscious *(point to it)*, is already programmed with everything you need to make your body work and live a life.

100 things to learn before you're 10

semi-conscious   *un-conscious*

conscious

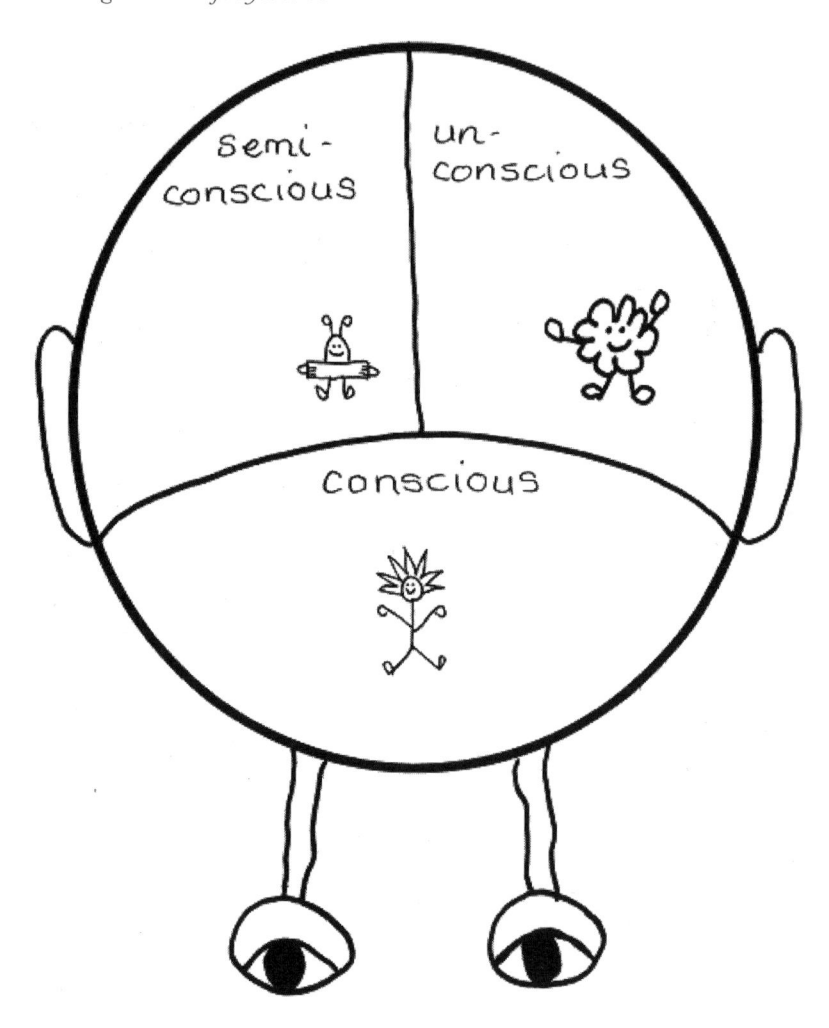

The helper in charge is awesome. I call him Deep. You cannot tell him anything, he knows it all already and just gets on with the job. Just as well really, because we've enough to do with living a life and developing everything else without having to think about breathing or growing or when we might be hungry. Deep already has it sorted and never fails to deliver, even on health he does a stirling job with his army of helpers. Pity he has to knock us out every night to do it, but there you go. That's Deep, for you, doesn't like interference. It's amazing engineering when you think about it.

The really exciting and important part that you need to know about though, is that the Conscious and the Semiconscious are **not** fully programmed when you're born but are **yours to train and develop** and use as you go through your life. Marvellous, isn't it? The thing is, your brain will work whether you use it or not, because it has a basic kind of setting, but if we want to excel and develop, we need to train our brain to work for **us** and let it know what we want it to do or it may become a nuisance and find its own entertainment, which could get in our way.

Now, the really important thing you need to know is that everything you do has an effect on your brain, absolutely everything. It knows when something is really important to you, **because you keep on doing it.**

An example of how to train your brain to work for you:

Learning Times Tables

'If you want to learn the 6x Table for example, what you need to do is write it down carefully - hot tip: Rummage will like it better if you do it in pretty colours - and then hold it up and read it out loud three times (once for each part of your brain) every day. That's it! Simple. Just make sure, all of your brain is listening when you do it.

It's even more interesting if you time it. Rummage loves to know how long the 'torture' is going to be (he does hate repetition but he can handle this without Whine because it takes LESS THAN THREE MINUTES! What's not to like?

And if you do this every day for one or two weeks, eventually Rummage will get so bored (remember, he hates repetition), that in the end, just before he calls Whine to complain, he realises you really want this stuff and hands it to Stock to put away. Simple. Stress free. Done. Yay!

The more boring it gets, the quicker it gets thrown into the back (to Stock), and put away and then you can learn the next one! When you have done this, **you** will **feel** a great sense of achievement because you will have trained your brain yourself to do what you want it to do - *and* you will know your times tables. How cool is that?!

You can do this with learning poems, or parts for plays or songs (Rummage likes singing!) or anything you choose. Your brain is an awesome piece of kit. Look after it!

Note of warning: remember though, your brain gets programmed with what you do over and over. If what you keep on doing is not what you want, or not very helpful, it will still keep it because it doesn't know what's good for you and what isn't. So, if you want to have neat handwriting, practise; if you want to be tidy; clear up every week, it's quite simple. Your brain hasn't been in the world before *either,* which is why you need to follow the best adult advice you can find, which is usually (me, if it is you!).. mum, dad and teachers.

Dazzle

> The 10 year old girl had struggled with writing all through primary school. She was approaching 11+ and was told by her school that she would need to work harder, read more, *stop being lazy* and improve her writing if she wanted to pass.
>
> However, sitting in the corner of the small family room she shared with her mother and sister, sat a full size harp. Petite though she was, this child was able to hear a piece of harp music just once and then sit down and play it, perfectly.
>
> This child was diagnosed with dyslexia. She also had low self esteem and was lacking in confidence.

The 5 year old could not sit still, did not make eye contact, needed to stride up and down and was a bundle of energy and activity who was into everything.

However, he loved to have Encyclopaedia Brittanica read to him at bedtime.

This child was born with health issues but nothing could outshine his brilliance in thinking or his thirst for knowledge. He was diagnosed at 6 years with dyslexia and dyspraxia. He was later assessed as being in the 'gifted and talented' range - and still found the physical process of writing difficult.

The exceptionally bright 7 year old boy just wasn't getting the hang of reading; he didn't enjoy doing it because it was 'hard' but he loved listening stories...

However, as the teacher took a breath to introduce and explain the next level of maths for him, he saw 984 + 67 = written on a piece of paper and immediately said, 'that's 1051' with a big grin. When asked how he had done it, he didn't know but said, 'my brain did it for me'.

This child was diagnosed with dyslexia. The psychologist who did the assessment told his parents that their son's frustration came from his high level of intelligence; saying it was like owning a Porche and driving it with the handbrake on.

These are just three examples of children who don't 'fit the mould' and whose achievements in academic life, do not reflect their high intelligence and talent. There are many such children. In fact, it is estimated that as much as 10% of the population will have a dyslexic brain; that means three children in every class of thirty children.

In their book 'The Dyslexic Advantage - Unlocking the hidden potential of the dyslexic brain', Drs. Brock and Fernette Eide inform us that ...*'dyslexic brains are organised in very different ways from most nondyslexic* brains because they're intended to work in different ways and to excel at different tasks'. They go on to specify the strengths of the dyslexic brain as follows

> *For dyslexic brains, excellent function typically means traits like the ability to see the gist or essence of things or to spot the larger context behind a given situation or idea; multidimensionality of perspective; the ability to see new, unusual or distant connections; inferential reasoning and ambiguity detection; the ability to recombine things in novel ways and a general inventiveness; and greater mindfulness and intentionality during tasks that others take for granted.*

From experience, children who have a dyslexic brain often have a surprisingly sharp and mischievous sense of humour; they are very quick-witted and keen to demonstrate their ways of solving problems. They can be very theatrical and entertaining; they can be deep and thoughtful and they will find solutions that are very creative whenever you ask them to help with a problem. Their spelling may be very weak and you may think they have learnt something one week and the next they seem to have forgotten it, but it is in a different context! Words read on one page and repeated on the next page may not be recognised because they are surrounded by different words on each page.

It is very likely, the child with a dyslexic brain cannot organise themselves until they are shown how and then reminded lots of times. They will often forget homework, reading book, pencil case, glasses, bags and P.E. kit. They don't mean to forget them, their brain is so busy, it 'slips their mind'. To help them, you need to do that part of the thinking for them and then show them what to do and remind them, often, until the pathways are established. It can take years. You will develop patience!

Read to them on a daily basis. Struggling to read by themselves can be so demoralising and until they are confident, encourage them to be 'an apprentice to an expert' - you. Sit alongside them so their brain can follow as you track the words for them by pointing along the line as you read. Remember, children aged 0-12 years are based in feeling. If they struggle with reading, they will come to hate it and their behaviour will deteriorate, even if they like listening to stories. So, make the experience a positive one. This will bolster them for the challenges they run into at school.

One difficulty faced by children who have a dyslexic brain, is that they are being educated in a system which is designed for the non-dyslexic brain. Their learning journey is therefore at least twice as challenging! Not only do they need to perform and deliver in the way that 'comes naturally' to the non-dyslexic brain, but that doesn't come naturally to them; they also need to deal with the fact they are unlikely to find the support they need to develop their special talents, which can be very frustrating for them. Any additional support tends to focus on helping them navigate their way through the education system. Added to this is the complication of the judgement and prejudice they meet at an early age, which often wreaks havoc with their self esteem and confidence.

Talking to your children about the Two Lives so that they use the world and school to develop themselves rather than see themselves at odds with some ideal they fail to conform to, can be very helpful. Explaining The Brain to them certainly helps. When you are describing the different sections of the brain, adding an extra little helper called Dazzle who can 'sometimes be a distraction for Stock' in the library, de-personalises it and helps the children see it as an added extra to be developed. Dazzle is the gift that needs to mature and find its unique talent for expression into the world. The books and games listed in this book can be used to develop and strengthen their working memory and organisation skills.

Remember to bear in mind the 'long view'. What does this child need to learn to be independent in the world? What can be done now, to help them develop the talent that dyslexia has given them? Give your child every opportunity to discover and develop their talent, it is where their satisfaction can be found and will be a boost to their self esteem and confidence.

Recommended reading about dyslexia for parents:

'The Dyslexic Advantage - Unlocking the hidden potential of the dyslexic brain', Dr. Brock Eide and Dr. Fernette Eide

Recommended reading for children who find reading a challenge:

In addition to the 50 Most Loved, Most Used, Most Useful Books for Children from 4 -12 years old selected from the Teacher's Personal Collection....listed at the end of this book, here are three more excellent series to consider:

Barrington Stoke Books - specialise in books for children with dyslexia

The 'Who Was' Series - very interesting and accessible text

Geronimo Stilton - great for teaching expression

Lesson 3:
Start Here

> A 9 year old boy, living with his estranged mum and grandma in difficult circumstances, needed to believe that this was not 'it'. That life would not always be the way it was at that moment and that things could improve, somehow. Start Here was created and revealed especially for this child. He will always remember it.

Start Here has continued to help so many children who need a boost to self esteem or confidence; or who have suffered with anxiety or confusion. It has helped heal over some of life's major difficult experiences, such as adoption and divorce, because it separates the child from the issue and acknowledges them as a valuable individual in their own right instead of feeling as though they are a victim.

Start Here is also, simply, a very beautiful, uplifting and empowering message to be told before you are 10 and has become a core lesson of benefit to all children for that reason. It may be kept for when a 'Mummy Moment' is needed.

A 'Mummy Moment' (doesn't depend on gender, could be a Daddy Moment as well) can happen when your child has run into a very real contradiction in themselves which has caused them to doubt everything they believed to that point and they need some help to figure it out.

Mummy Moments are when you and your child connect 'human to human'; 'real' things get discussed and you both understand each other. It doesn't happen often and you both know it's very special. You feel strongly protective. Your child soaks up that protection and help and feels less vulnerable because of it.

To help create the right atmosphere, it is best to sit side by side with your child and look at a notepad and blank piece of paper. Talk slowly and deliberately to give your child's brain time to process these words. As you speak the words below, let their brain watch as you sketch each item that you are speaking about. (The artwork doesn't need to be perfect!) Pause, where you feel pauses are needed. Make it special.

Alternatively, or on a different occasion, tell your child to close their eyes and imagine it all as you read it slowly and deliberately…it makes a great, confirming little meditation before finishing the day.

Begin like this…

'The year before you were born…

the planet was here.

(draw a circle on your paper)

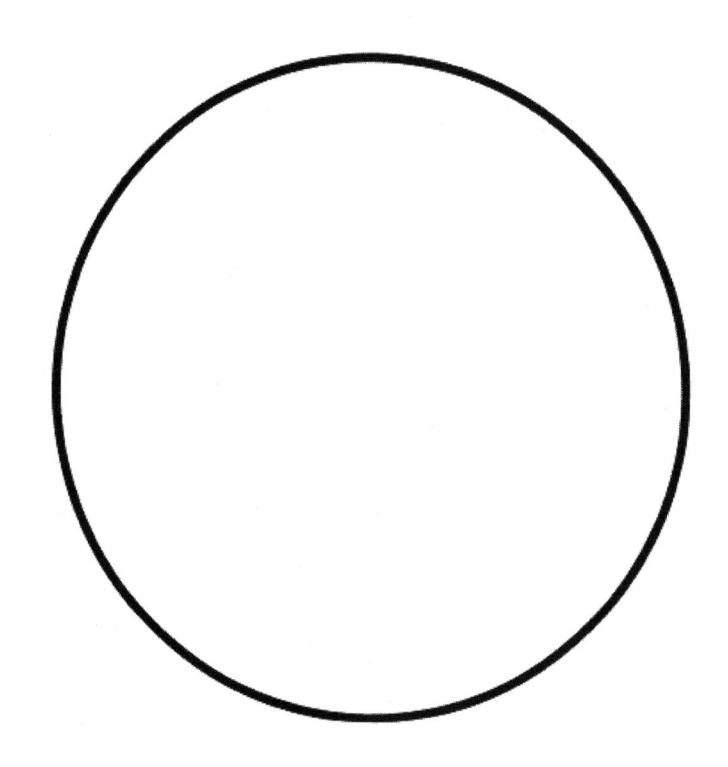

100 things to learn before you're 10

It had countries on it.

(add a few country-type shapes in your circle)

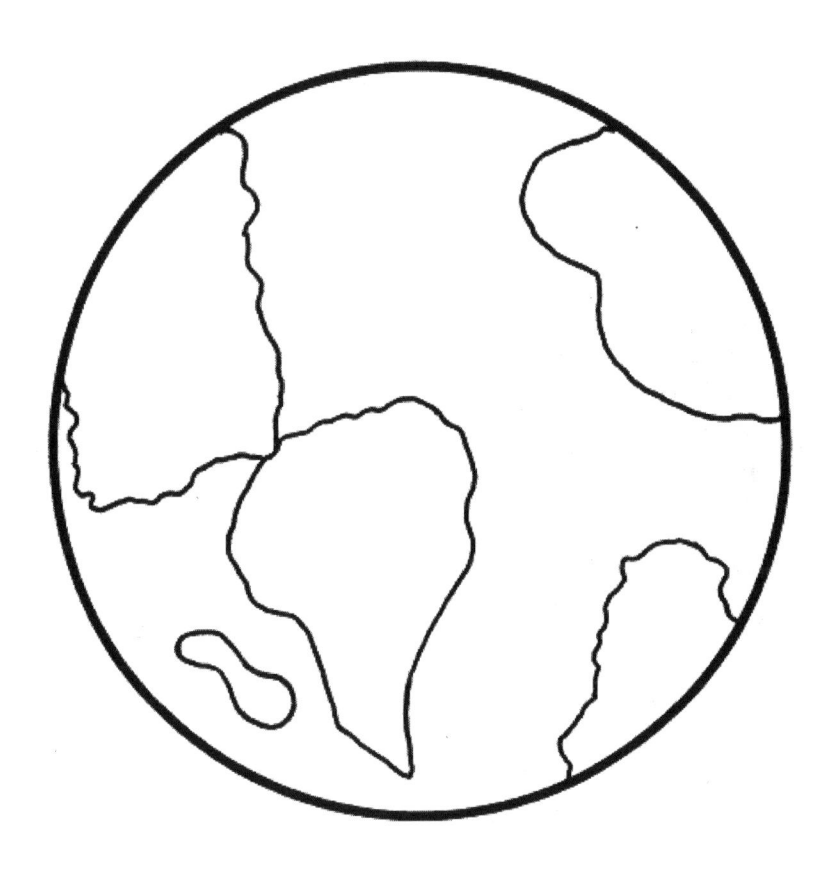

39

100 things to learn before you're 10

It had trees on it.

(add a token tree...)

100 things to learn before you're 10

It had flowers on it

100 things to learn before you're 10

and giraffes,

elephants,

birds, bees and butterflies…

(continue to add items to your drawing as you feel appropriate)

There were houses.

(continue adding to the illustration as you talk….you don't need to add everything…it is the process *that is important, not the drawing…)*

Lots of houses…

boats, fish and bicycles

ants, aeroplanes, donkeys….

and

6, 873, 219, 421

(six billion, eight hundred and seventy three million, two hundred and nineteen thousand, four hundred and twenty one)

people on it.

Your mum *(say 'I' if you are talking to your own child!)* was here, *(draw simple stick-figure 'mum' somewhere on land)*

Your dad was here too, *(draw 'dad' next to mum)*

but you hadn't been created yet.

100 things to learn before you're 10

Everything was working as it does today…

and it was

busy

(as it is today).
(make some 'busy' squiggles on your picture)

Then,

you arrived.
(draw 'baby' somewhere on planet…)

and changed the world.

Forever.

And you can see things are not quite right here.

And you can make it better or worse by what you do.

We would love you to help make it better.

You can do this every day in every little thing you do.

Start now.

Watch the animation of **Start Here** at www.lessonsalive.com (Blog)

Poem:
We see the trees and flowers

We see the trees and flowers
And know to make them grow
We need to feed and tend them
In drought they will be slow

We see a snowflake falling
Each one unique and new
We know to look for patterns
Nature's giving us the clue

And when each life arrives here
It's fresh and clean and bright
Look in the eyes of each young child
A most refreshing sight

And yet it is so fragile
So easy to distort
Because, you see, they're open
To everything they're taught

We must preserve this freshness
Taking care in all we do
And not confuse the system
But keep it good as new

100 things to learn before you're 10

Lesson 4:
Time

Key point to remember: brains are built to work with facts. They like things to be specific, exact, precise! Children need to know: 'There are 24 hours in a day. People who do really well in life have 24 hours in their day. People who don't do well also have 24 hours in their day. How well we do can depend on how we use those 24 hours…'

While we are used to using phrases like:

- 'hang on a minute'

- 'I won't be a moment'

- 'it'll take 5 minutes'

- 'just a second'

- 'I won't be long'

and we know what we mean, basically, that whatever we're talking about is not going to take very much time; this does not give a young, developing brain the **reference** it needs to understand the concept of time, which is crucial to the child learning to plan, organise and work efficiently for themselves.

To give your child's brain a reference point for time: use a one minute timer they can see easily (it is important the brain is watching at the same time!). The best kind of timer for a young brain is a large, sand timer. The brain can't miss that! Showing them the timer, say to your child:

'We're going to see how long a minute really is…stand 'here' *(point to a specific spot - to make it graphic for the brain to remember)* Put your hands on your shoulders *(or stand on one leg, but they are often distracted by*

100 things to learn before you're 10

wobbling!) we're going to see how long a minute is. Just stand there like that, don't say anything and watch the timer. Ready? *When they nod or say they're ready, tell them:* Turning on, now.'

Ignoring all distractions, watch the timer together with your child and afterwards ask them what it felt like; was it a short time or a long time?

Explain what we mean when we say, 'hang on a minute' and other similar phrases.

Have some fun reinforcing 'a minute' with these exercises: ALWAYS use the timer for this and ALWAYS let your child see the timer and let them *know what they are learning* by doing the exercise.

Can you be **completely** silent for one minute? Yes or no? Self control takes practise. The children need to know this. If they have not grasped the concept of 'minute' they may think that they can easily be quiet for 'a minute', but only when they try will they discover the truth! The way to learn this is through practise. By alternating one minute silent with one minute 'as noisy as you like' (block your ears, folks!) and by being exact in the timing, children can find it fun to learn self control!

> When asked if he had ever taken control of his body, the 7 year old boy looked surprised, giggled and said he could. In a lighthearted way, he was dared to show this control and to keep still for one minute. He accepted the dare. A timer was set. After 10 seconds the boy giggled and wriggled, realising that he could not do it! He took a deep breath and said he was sure he could do it, so he was given another chance. The timer was set. The boy sat up really straight, determined not to give in and stared directly ahead, hardly daring to breathe. When the minute was up, he heaved a huge sigh of relief and completely flopped in the chair. He was given a round of applause and everyone went back about what they were doing before this little interlude. After a short pause, when all attention had left him, the boy quietly threw down the gauntlet again and muttered, 'I could do it for 3 minutes'.

> OK, This was Game On! This time he relaxed into it and sat perfectly composed and with ease, for a full 3 minutes. His obvious achievement was congratulated by all present. Two days later, with enormous delight, he ran home to tell his mother that his teacher had given him a certificate at school, 'for excellent concentration'...

More ways to help your child appreciate 'a minute' and learn more about themselves and what they are capable of:

1. How many jumps do you think you can do in one minute? (Important: estimate first, then find out!). By doing this you will teach your brain what you are able to do (which will change as you grow and develop). It helps you to see what is real for you; brains can sometimes overestimate!

2. Let's see how many times can you write your name in a minute, what do you think? (Important: estimate first then find out with a piece of paper and a pencil). This will show your brain how much you can actually write in a minute - it needs to know this so that it can help you plan work, get work finished in time and not waste time.

3. Can you catch the ball or juggle (depending on age), for a minute without dropping the ball(s)?

4. Can you skip for one minute? This makes the muscles in your legs stronger, helps you build stamina and helps you be in control of yourself

5. How many steps can you walk in one minute? Do you know? Let's try! If you want to do more, practise speeding yourself up and then time it again next week

6. Trace a picture for one minute. While you do this, you can let your brain know that you want to be able to be careful with your work and you want it to follow directions when you decide it should

7. Run on the spot for one minute. This helps to develop your body's skills, balance and coordination and strengthens your muscles.

8. Hit a target with a ball, stone, dart or rolled up piece of paper. This helps your hands and eyes work together which is important for many skills like cutting with a knife or scissors, or throwing, sewing, picking up small things….

9. Look at the sky (or an object you choose) for one minute. This helps to improve your observation and teaches your brain attention to detail.

Children find all these mini challenges fun to do when no pressure is put on them. If they are trying to speed up in work, this kind of exercise is a very helpful one that doesn't judge or pressure from outside but lets your child 'judge' and pressure themselves from the inside. They love it and will set little challenges for themselves. Great for motivation and achievement!

Using Time

> An 8 year old boy was resenting the fact that he had to do homework after school and there were often arguments about it at home, upsetting everyone involved. He felt as though his whole life was being dominated by school and work and was resisting it every step of the way.

The Using Time lesson helped to change his attitude to homework; his perception of school and his enthusiasm for getting work done. It has since become a core lesson because it is such an effective tool, used and adapted frequently for changing attitude, levels of satisfaction and encouraging independence and organisation. It can be adapted for use wth children from 5 up to ……adult!

You will need some paper, a pencil and your child's school timetable: Sit alongside your child and ask as follows:

100 things to learn before you're 10

'How many hours are there in a day?' *Establish that there are 24 hours in a day.*

'When does the day start? I mean, when did it stop being *(whatever yesterday was e.g. Monday)* and start being *(whatever today is, Tuesday)*?'

Most children do figure out that the day 'starts' at midnight, but if your child doesn't know, now is the time to tell them!

As you establish that the day starts at midnight: write it on the top line of the paper like this:

00:00

Then ask:

'What are you doing when the day starts?'

Mostly, of course, they will say 'sleeping' and you write that onto the paper alongside 00:00.

00:00　　　　　　**Sleeping**

Then ask:

'What are you doing an hour later at 1 o'clock in the morning?'

Write it underneath 00:00 on the paper (it's best to leave a line so that there is plenty of space and the child's brain can assimilate all the information as you develop it…you mustn't rush through this or the point will not be made).

00:00　　　　　　**Sleeping**

01:00　　　　　　**Sleeping**

'What are you doing at 2 am?' *Add it to the paper…*

100 things to learn before you're 10

00:00	**Sleeping**
01:00	**Sleeping**
02:00	**Sleeping**

'3 am?' *Add to the paper...*

00:00	**Sleeping**
01:00	**Sleeping**
02:00	**Sleeping**
03:00	**Sleeping**

'04:00?' *Add to the paper...*

00:00	**Sleeping**
01:00	**Sleeping**
02:00	**Sleeping**
03:00	**Sleeping**
04:00	**Sleeping**

and then continue by saying:

'What you may not know, is that up until this time, it is dark in this country, while you are asleep. At about 4 o'clock it starts very slowly to get light and by about half past 4 or quarter to five, the energy from the sun wakes up all the birds and they start singing very loudly! We call this part of the day Dawn and the birds singing is called the Dawn Chorus. What are you doing at 5 o'clock?

Still sleeping? Gosh, you sleep a lot don't you?!' *Add to the paper:*

00:00	**Sleeping**
01:00	**Sleeping**
02:00	**Sleeping**
03:00	**Sleeping**
04:00	**Sleeping**

Dark up to here but starting to get a little bit light….birds sing…and then go back to sleep'

05:00	**Sleeping'**

From this point, it can vary. Some children wake up at 6am and some not until 7am so you continue to ask, hour by hour what your child is doing at each hour until you complete the 24 hours, ready for the next stage of this discussion.

It's important to be methodical and **lead your child's brain** through this process. While you are doing this, your child's brain is making connections and collecting reference which will help them enormously to grasp the concept of time. Please don't take shortcuts. There aren't any!

EXAMPLE ON PAPER:

00:00	**Sleeping**
01:00	**Sleeping**
02:00	**Sleeping**
03:00	**Sleeping**
04:00	**Sleeping**

Dark up to here but starting to get a little bit light....birds sing...and then go back to sleep!

05:00	**Sleeping**
06:00	**Sleeping**
07:00	**Wake up**

Get up? Wash? Breakfast? TV? (some do!) what does your child DO between 7 am and 8 am - note it on the paper

08:00	**Leave for school**
09:00	**Start school**
10:00	**Lesson**
Break -	**20 minutes**
11:00	**Lesson**
12:00	**Lesson**
13:00	**Lunch and playtime**
14:00	**Lesson**
15:00	**Lesson**
16:00	**Clubs**
17:00	**Home**

Snack? Homework? Play? Read? Playdate?

| 18:00 | **Dinner** |

19:00	TV? Play? Reading? Homework?	

Getting dark again?

20:00	**Get ready for bed**	
21:00	**Bed**	
22:00	**Sleeping**	
23:00	**Sleeping**	
24:00	**Sleeping**	… End of day

When you have finished going through and recording the hours of the day, add up with your child:

How many hours they spend sleeping. How many hours they spend in lessons (NOT at school, but in actual lessons - the brain responds to FACTS). Most children are in actual lessons for between four and half and six hours per day (NOT ALL day as they think!)

Then, remind your child that there are 24 hours in the day; take away the hours sleeping (can be up to 12 for some children) and tell them how many hours are left.

Example:

'According to this, you sleep for 10 hours, if we take that away from 24 hours, that leaves you 14 hours.

If we take away time in lessons which is (for example) 6 hours, that leaves 8 hours to do everything else.

If we take away 2 hours for eating; washing; brushing teeth; dressing; that leaves 6 hours…

So, we've counted learning at school; sleeping, eating and washing and so on and taken them away and **you still have 6 hours left in every day** to do what you want to do, SO even if we took another hour every day to work on preparing you for doing well in school and in life by doing your homework and what you need to do to practise musical instruments and so on, that still leaves you with 5 hours out of 24 hours to play; watch tv and do all the things you want to do AND still get your work done. What do you think?'

Doing a session on time in this way, will help your child to put school and homework in perspective. They can be shown in a way that helps them realise that actually, they can separate in their mind, school from home and from 'the rest of my life'. Using this, you can teach them to appreciate structure far more; to challenge themselves to do a better job in the time they have and to become more efficient.

This exercise can be used to reinforce listening and concentration by examining how much time they are expected to **actually** listen (not the whole lesson, just about 20 minutes) and how long at any one time they are expected to concentrate. Done properly, it really is a useful exercise which can be adapted for many uses.

When children need to speed up their work rate:

> An intelligent, seven year old girl was a friendly, chatty, helpful girl who really loved school but was beginning to recognise that she was one of the slowest in her class and it was starting to bother her, her teacher and her parents, because she had begun to underperform and underachieve. This was solved with the following exercise in two separate sessions. It has worked for many other children from ages 7 - 10 years since.

Use a 2 minute timer, a picture that has lots of identical things to colour (see following example) and a range of nice, sharp colouring pencils:

Picking up the timer, say to your child:

'This is a two minute timer. We are going to **watch** as it runs for two minutes and when it is finished, I am going to ask you how many of these (point to pictures), you could colour, neatly, keeping in the lines with each section a different colour and showing no white bits. How many do you think you could colour like that in 2 minutes? Let's watch the timer while you think.'

Watch the timer together. When time is up, ask again how many they think they can colour and then, putting on the timer again, let them do it.

To start with it is likely they will only manage one or two whole 'bugs' and they may have thought they could colour more.

If they colour less than they anticipated; ask them what slowed them down. If they don't know, make a suggestion (one at a time, so that the brain has a chance to reflect). Ask them if they think there is anything they can do to speed up.

Very often, the children will not stop to count how many pencils they need to do the job and some of the time is lost choosing pencils.

If they think that was the reason, ask them to count how many pencils they need and get them ready. Then suggest they put all the others out of the way.

Try the 2 minute colouring exercise again to see if they can do more.

If they do more, point out the positive difference made by getting the pencils ready and ask if they think they could do even more...

You might point out that they chose the right number of pencils but then picked them up, used them and put them down again in the same place so they lost track of which ones they have used and which they hadn't.

Don't interfere in the process and tell them what to do - but ask leading questions, make observations so that you help them work it out and they get the development of it.

Afterwards, you can show them to pick up the first one, use it, put it 'over here' away from the others so you don't lose track. When they are ready, time them again to see if it helps them to do more.

These details all show your child what is slowing them down so doing this exercise is an opportunity for them to discover and for you to show and teach them what it means to organise themselves and how much more they can achieve when they do.

Each time the child 'has another go' at colouring for two minutes, ask them what they discover about their capabilities, about what slows them down and what speeds them up; about how they concentrate and how much control they can have over their work. It's a very valuable exercise for all sorts of reasons. Focus on one thing at a time for real development and change.

The children start by colouring just one or two bugs and after going through this process, normally finish by completing more. What you need to point out to them is that **you** did nothing to make them faster. Whatever went on inside them made them faster, whether it was being more focused, more organised or more efficient, **they need your reflection to help them realise** and 'seal' the development that can happen through this process by congratulating them. This is what is meant by positive praise! The children know they've achieved something and they feel great!

When the exercise is finished, go over what your child has learnt so that you help them to **realise** (make real) the learning : e.g.

- My brain overestimates how quickly I do things so I must allow more time

- Preparation makes me more efficient

- It helps to have everything ready so that I can just get on with the job

- Being organised makes me quicker

- When I am organised I can use my energy to do the job and not have to keep working out 'what next' or looking for something I need.

It's very important to confirm to them - and to their brain - that improvement is something they can do by themselves and if ever they are not sure **how** to improve, they need to ask you or their teacher.

The card game Blink is an excellent, brilliantly fun game for helping speed up mental process.

100 things to learn before you're 10

60

Lesson 5: Listening

> When asked if he knew what listening meant, the 6 year old nodded his head, crossed his arms triumphantly, put his index finger up to seal his lips, glanced at his brother and giggled.

He obviously had no idea what listening actually meant and it is the same for most children.

Here are some facts about listening:

When we listen to someone speaking, we get:

- 55% of a message's meaning from the person's facial expression

- 38% from how he or she says the message

- 7% from the words actually spoken

- We listen to people at a rate of 125 - 250 words per minute, but we think at 1,000 - 3,000 words per minute.

- Many workers send and receive about 1,800 messages a day

- Banking employees spend 80% of their time communicating with others either individually or in groups.

That means 48 minutes in every hour!

The No.1 quality employers want: Communication skills. A survey showed it is more important than ambition, education and hard work!

Only around 2% of the population ever have any form of training in listening and yet it is one of the most important skills we need for learning; for understanding others, for empathy and for personal development!

Teaching your child to listen

> A father was shocked as he listened (outside the room), while his bright, articulate 9 year old son was asked to repeat a sentence exactly as it was spoken.
>
> Apart from the boy and the teacher, there were no other people in the quiet room and no external distractions.
>
> Here is the sentence the boy was asked to repeat... Before I went outside, I put on my jacket.
>
> Child first try: *Before I went out I put my jacket on*
>
> Sentence repeated: Before I went outside, I put on my jacket
>
> Child second try: *Before I went outside, I got my jacket*
>
> Sentence repeated: Before I went outside, I put on my jacket
>
> Child third try: *Before I went out to play, I put my jacket on....*
>
> It took eight attempts. It was attempt four before the boy realised that it was not as easy as he thought; it was attempt six before he realised he wasn't listening properly; stopped giggling and tried to focus. It was the eighth attempt when he succeeded in repeating the sentence as it was spoken to him.

This is important because it shows what the brain does with the information as it comes in. Most of the time, we interpret the incoming information and manage to get the 'gist' of a message but there are times when accuracy is needed if the brain is to create the correct connections for us to develop a skill.

From birth-12years is when we establish the early frameworks in the brain that determine the quality of our foundation for life. Accuracy is important.

What children need to know about listening - reference that is helpful for the brain and how to develop the skill

Development does not happen overnight. These messages are core to children's understanding of listening but you might need to have several conversations about it as they learn.

It's impossible for a child to remember all of these in one go but they are put here for parents' reference when they are focusing on their child's listening skill. You will need to return to them often.

Whenever possible, whatever you are teaching, give your child examples from your own experience and point out examples that you know about in *their* experience (e.g. you remember when we were at Aunty Betty's and….happened'). This helps to consolidate and reference the connections in the brain.

You need to begin by defining what you are talking about.

- Hearing happens, but listening is something we need to **do**

- Listening is a skill

- Because it is a skill, it means we can get better at it

- When we listen we use all our attention to focus on what is being said

- When we listen properly, our brain starts to make connections (like dot-to-dot) with things that we already know and this helps us to understand what is being said

- Everything we do uses energy, absolutely everything; we know running uses energy and jumping uses energy but so does moving even just a little bit.

- Sleeping uses energy, not very much, but it still uses energy and so do thinking and listening.

- This means that if you are listening to someone, you probably need to keep your body still or quiet so that the energy you need to listen isn't being used by fidgeting about!

- Our brains get information from all our senses

- When we are trying to listen to someone we mostly use hearing, but our brains want to **see** the lips and face of the person speaking to make sure we are hearing correctly; so we need to look at the person speaking to us

- Sounds are energy that we cannot see and when someone speaks to us, they are giving us a little bit of energy.

- When we look at the person talking, it is easier for us to get the energy so that we don't have to say 'pardon' and make them have to do it all again

- When you listen to people, they feel like they matter and they like that

- Good listening shows you are in control of yourself which makes you look mature

- When you manage yourself, you have more energy for the things you want to do

- Being a good listener builds patience and empathy in you and these are qualities that can help your life in general

- If you are a good listener, other people will be encouraged to listen to you and that will help you to feel understood which is always a good feeling

- Remember that your conscious brain gets easily distracted so you have to decide to listen and make yourself focus

- Listening can be difficult if there is a lot of noise around you, but not impossible

- Your brain can get easily distracted by things happening while you are listening (refer to Rummage if you have done the Brain Lesson)

- Your brain hears so much during the day and it doesn't really know what matters and what doesn't matter which is why you don't remember it all

- If something is important, like at school or something your parents are telling you, you can help your brain to keep it by repeating inside your head so that it gets put away

Activities for teaching Listening to your child

A seven year old boy was asked what was beeping as he tried to work at the kitchen table. 'I've lived here all my life (all seven years) and I've always wondered that, too', he replied...what he needed was reference to settle his brain.

The Sound Maker Hunt

Tell your child you're going on a Soundmaker hunt to find out how many things in your home make a sound: a) sometimes and b) constantly.

Tell them you're going to do this so that:

1. they are able to recognise the sounds whether or not they can see where they are coming from so their brain won't need to struggle to identify them

2. they will know which ones mean they need to do something and which don't (include alarms, such as the freezer, and tell them what they need to do if they hear them).

Choose a starting point e.g. your own front door.

- Actively look for everything that makes a sound and make it work : eg. door opening/closing, key in lock, postbox, bell, knocker etc.

- Move through your home, room by room, identifying the Sound Makers - operate all the drawers, switches, handles etc. look in cupboards…. you are making your child's brain conscious of the actions connected with the sounds in the home. The will help your child to be calmer and more confident.

- Brains like to know things at this age - they are looking for reference. Everything is on 'ALERT' when we hear a noise we don't recognise – this can be very unsettling for children (especially at night).

> In the open plan room, an eight year old was focusing on homework at the dining table, his mother was busy out of sight round a corner, in the kitchen. There was a curious sound from the kitchen area and the boy's brain had no reference for it so it remained a distraction from his work. Finally, he simply *had* to get up to see what his mum was doing! Once his brain could associate the image of his mother finely chopping (lots of) onions with the sound he could hear, he was able to focus on his work again.

Activity:
The Jumpasound

This activity is often hugely enjoyable! Tell your child you are going to give them a listening challenge! They need to get ready to leap about, laugh, giggle, sing, clap their hands and LISTEN (all at the same time if they like)! Tell them that while they are leaping about, you are going to say a sentence to them (one at a time, please!) but there is a rule and it is this:

When you have finished speaking and clapped your hands, they must repeat the sentence back to you accurately and exactly, word for word, <u>as you spoke it</u>! Do not compromise!

Here are a few sentences to get you going – don't always simplify!

- Jonathan likes to read books about elephants

- The big dog looked fierce but he was playful

- The washing machine is being repaired tomorrow

- I put my jacket on to go out to play

For a more challenging exercise, use a series of numbers

- 7, 4, 3, 2

- 9, 7, 2, 5

- 8, 4, 9, 1

Focus: Apart from being fun, the results of this exercise can enable you to discuss and reflect at a deeper level on:

1. Whether they can move and listen effectively at the same time

2. Whether they need eye contact for effective listening

3. And whether or not their focus is affected by movement and distraction

Activity:
The Back to Back Book

Choose a new and interesting picture book for this exercise and explain to your child that you're going to do an activity together to show them how important it is to be involved in the process of listening. To do this, you're going to read a story to them but first you must sit back to back so you cannot see each other and they cannot see the book.

You read the picture book slowly. After the first four pages, ask the child what is happening in them.

- Are they enjoying the story?

- Are they enjoying the experience?

- Would they prefer to be face to face?

If the answer is 'yes' to the last question, which is likely, tell them you will turn around but not show the pictures to them yet. Read four more pages. Ask the child what that's like and how they feel. Share the end of the book. Remember, your focus is listening, don't be sidetracked by the story!

By talking about their responses, help the child to realise:

- Listening is to do with more than hearing

- Pictures and expressions matter when we are listening because they add more information to help us understand

- The speaker gets more pleasure from speaking if someone is listening

Activity:
The Outside Sounds - investigations...

Consciously and deliberately, for the purpose of gathering reference for your child's brain, take a couple of minutes when you are in a supermarket to discover the sounds you can hear *only* in a supermarket....or..

1. In an airport

2. In a car park

3. In a hospital

4. In a library

5. In a church

6. In the park

7. In a swimming pool

8. At the playground

9. In a cemetery

10. At the zoo

Try listening with eyes closed and open…make it interesting and encourage your child to put language on the different sounds so that their vocabulary increases. By doing this, you will be helping your child build the foundation for descriptive creative writing as well as building their confidence; helping them feel settled in their surroundings.

Freddie and the Fairy by Julia Donaldson is a great book for helping to teach your child to listen carefully (and speak clearly!).

Lesson 6:
THE BUBBLE STRATEGY

or how to encourage your child to take control of their listening (or concentration or focus) at school when you are not there!

Children love having a strategy that helps them focus in the classroom. This one is called the Bubble Strategy and it can be easily taught to any age child. It takes about 10 minutes to teach and can last a lifetime.

Choose a time when there will be minimal distraction. Tell the child to sit comfortably, ready to learn something that may be very useful to help with listening. It is a very useful tool when we are trying to concentrate as well. You can play some nice music in the background if you wish.

Ask them to relax, reassure them that no-one is going to touch them or their things so they can close their eyes to help them concentrate and imagine better.

Speaking evenly and softly, instruct your child to imagine themselves inside a big, invisible bubble. Only they can see it from the inside. It can be any colour they like and it goes all around the outside of them. Wait while they do this.

If the child has difficulty visualising this, suggest they have a helpful little 'friend' standing on their head who is going to help them by using a pot of brightly coloured paint. Slowly, they pour the paint out of the pot and it trickles down around them until they are surrounded in the colour.

As they go into their classroom, they do this exercise in their heads and imagine themselves inside their bubble. When they are in their bubble, the only thing they can hear is their teacher or the person who is meant to be talking. All other noise is outside the bubble and in the distance.

As soon as the lesson is finished, they can shake off the bubble (do a whole body shake or just wave it away with a hand) and go to break. During break they can run around and play with their friends as much as they like.

Let them know that they don't need their bubble all the time, only when they are in the classroom. As soon as they go back into the classroom they will need to put their bubble up again for the next lesson.

Next time your child goes to school, remind them to try this strategy. Suggest they try it for the first lesson to see how they get on.

When they come home again, ask how it went with the bubble. Make adjustments if necessary e.g. sometimes children say that someone 'came inside my bubble' – they need to know that they can repair the bubble by themselves if there is an intruder!

Use a link such as a bubble sticker on their pencil case or a pretty shell or stone in their pencil case. Tell them that every time they see it, in or on their pencil case, it will help to remind them to use their bubble.

> A 10 year old boy who had been given the bubble strategy went on to get more and more success in his work and school life. He was paying better attention, had a greatly improved attitude, was much happier in himself and was raising his exam scores. When he was asked if he still used the bubble when he was in the classroom, he said it had somehow become 'automatic'....

Sixteen questions to ask yourself and reflect on if your child does not listen:

1. Did I get their attention first (by name, by touch, by being in the same room)?
2. Did I interrupt a process (they were concentrating on something else; they were in a conversation)?
3. Can they hear me (over headphones, over the TV, over the traffic; or ear problems: glue ear, sinus infection)?
5. Did I stop them and make eye contact first?
6. Do they understand the difference between hearing and listening?
7. Am I speaking too quickly? (VERY common)
8. Am I saying too much? Too many words? (this is a huge problem in many child/parent relationships)
9. Am I speaking clearly?
10. Have they got time to think about what I have said and respond?
11. Do I frequently make idle threats?
    If you say it and then not follow up and do it; they will switch off!
12. Do I repeat myself over and over again? Say it, mean it, do it!
13. Are they sleeping well?
14. Does what I'm saying match my body language and what they are feeling from me? (words do not mask what is really going on in us!)
15. Are you allowing them thinking and response time?
16. Have you got a signal you can use to say 'I see you but now is not a good moment', - a hand gesture? a nod?

100 things to learn before you're 10

Lesson 7:
A little bit about the learning process… older children (7+) love to know!

> A Year 4 class were very excited and fascinated the day the farmer came into school to talk to them. He brought vegetables from his farm and he talked about how they were grown and harvested. He let the children taste the food and answered lots of questions. It was a very enjoyable, busy day. After he left, the children were asked what they had learned from the day. 'Farmers wear earrings', they chorused….'and he was so cool, Miss'!

If the children don't realise they're learning then it is highly likely they are *not* learning what you *think* they are learning! Which is why your commentary and feedback about what they are *doing* is so important. What **you** say helps the developing brain to build the connections that lead to realisation. When you see that your child has achieved a new connection (because of what they say and do), then you can congratulate them which confirms it is correct. They get a feeling of satisfaction and achievement. It is such a good feeling that it helps to 'cement' the attitude so that motivation becomes self perpetuating and success breeds success.

Recent developments in neuroscience tell us that when we **decide** to learn something new, we create pathways in our brain. These are called neural pathways. With repetition, the brain gets the message that this is something we want to keep so it coats the pathway in a substance called myelin. Myelin protects the pathway so that we remember how to do the action automatically. The more repetition there is, the more the brain produces myelin which protects the connections we have made.

Summarising Daniel Coyle in his (highly recommended) book: The Talent Code, just 'going through the motions' does not create the pressure needed to develop these pathways; **motivation** is critical to the process of myelin production. We have to want to or **decide** to do it.

The question parents and teachers really need to ask is: What is this child actually learning? What pathway is being created in the brain?

If you have the right attitude and motivation, learning really is straightforward and a real pleasure.

To have the right motivation and attitude we need:

- A *core* reason for the action - what is this doing for my natural life; what is it helping me to develop?

- What am I trying to achieve? What will 'success' look like?

- How do I get there? What are the steps I need to take?

- An example of what success can look like…reference in the brain

- A real enthusiasm, curiosity and drive to develop

By allocating just 5-10 minutes a day (timed), to specifically focus on helping your child develop myelin you can make a great difference. It can be helpful to use homework focusing on one particular aspect (see Homework section) - or practicing a musical instrument - for this purpose. You can also interpret activities they naturally enjoy - such as building Lego, tracing, colouring or helping and identify what pathway or skill they are trying to establish and help them. The motivation and tools are already there from birth.

> A 7 year old girl was trying to improve her handwriting. She was shown exactly how to form the letters of a word as *the commentary for doing it was spoken.*
>
> 'Start on the line, go all the way up here, that's the join. Next, you need to make the letter, go straight back down to the line, back to the middle, over and round and out, ready for the next join...' (That

> is the commentary for the letter b with a lead in)
>
> She tried to do what she had seen....at the same time, the same commentary was spoken aloud to her because the formation of the letter and the neural pathway was not yet established in her brain... 'Start on the line, go all the way ...no, no, all the way to here...ok, leave that and start again on the next line...'
>
> She had no way to correct it herself yet and if she continued, her brain would not build the neural pathway correctly. For this reason the commentary was repeated four or five times as she wrote, until she 'got it'.

This is the learning process. The targets were small and easy to achieve. 'Start on the line… Go all the way up here…' Once her brain had made the correct neural pathway, she was *naturally* thrilled with her work, confident she could achieve it again and again (because the pathway to do with the letter b was now correctly created) and the actual writing on the paper was the evidence that the process had been successfully accomplished. This was confirmed and congratulated by all the adults around as being *genuinely* 'brilliant, well done!'

100 things to learn before you're 10

100 things to learn before you're 10

Lesson 8:
Concentration

> The 11 year old boy had a history of disruptive behaviour and underachievement at his private school, so much so, an assistant was employed to sit with him in the classroom so that he could be kept on task. However, the assistant was leaving to have a baby and the school had informed the boy's parents that unless a replacement supervisor could be found, he would need to find another school. The situation was urgent. September was looming and no replacement support had been found.

When there are few options left; it is necessary to get responsibly creative!

First, it was important to make sure that this boy understood what 'concentration' actually *means*: he was asked to walk on a one-brick deep edge that ran along the sides of the lawn in the garden. At first, he giggled; lost his balance and went back to the start. After a few attempts, he got the timing and balance right and was able to walk along the lawn edging, watching where he was putting his feet.

At the point where it was clear he was focused, he was told quite specifically: *'What you are now feeling is called 'concentration'. All of your energy is aimed at doing one thing and you are not allowing anything to distract you.'*

On the next border walk; he was told to continue to walk as he had been and to repeat these words over and over out loud for his brain: *I am walking the path of focus and concentration. I am walking the path of focus and concentration....*

The boy was then advised that he should imagine himself on the same path and to repeat the same words to himself as he walked up the school drive each day.

To help him in the classroom, a sticking plaster (a link), was put on the back of his hand with the instruction that every time he looked at

79

it, it would remind him to take charge in himself and not let himself be distracted.

At the same time, the school were made aware of the action being taken and asked to support it if he was becoming disruptive by reminding him about the walk and what the plaster was for; to reflect back the new expectation whenever he lapsed into habitual behaviour and continue the same feedback and commentary that would help him establish a new pattern of behaviour. Each evening, he would telephone the learning mentor to review his behaviour for that day, receive encouraging and reinforcing messages and plan targets for the next day. Although it would be lovely to report it was plain sailing, that wouldn't be accurate!

It was very tough for all concerned because of the habits the boy had already developed which needed to be changed or managed; because of the expectations of his parents and a school staff weary of years of disruptive and cheeky behaviour and because of goading from other pupils whenever he tried to be different.

However, as the weeks went by, his behaviour *did* improve sufficiently that the 'three month probation' imposed by the school was lifted and he went on to achieve a pass in all exams, despite his diagnosed, but now managed, 'mild dyslexia', which may have been the initial trigger for his lack of focus when he was much younger.

Until puberty, children are based in feeling. *Experiencing* concentration, *feeling* what it is like and **giving that feeling a name** is a vital reference for the brain to know how to respond and behave at school or whenever concentration is needed.

Defining Concentration for your child (reference)

- Concentration is a skill. That means it is something we can control.

- Being mesmerised is not necessarily the same as concentrating. Different things are happening in the brain. Remember from the 'brain lesson', Rummage loves new, colourful, bright things and can easily be mesmerised (e.g. by screens!)

- Sometimes, concentrating is easy, especially when we really want to learn something. But sometimes, it may need effort because there are distractions around. We have to be in control and decide to focus all our energy.

- Having a good reason to do something helps us to develop concentration when we are learning. If you are not sure why you are doing something, ask what it will help you to develop so that your brain knows the reason.

- Concentration uses energy and we can feel quite tired after we concentrate so we need to take a brain break; such as juggling; drinking water; walking about and getting fresh air; having a snack….keep it short, but simple. (A list of brain breaks is included in the book)

Daily starter: to develop and strengthen concentration skills:

This plan is for 10 minutes before school each morning for at least one week, but can go on throughout the school year or until a good level of concentration has been reached.

The starter can be shortened or extended according to age by removing or adding minutes in the second section, but needs to be at least 5 minutes and no more than 15 minutes. Substitute and change activities as the weeks go on but **ALWAYS TIMED**.

- **Start: 2 minute warm up each day: 1 minute each exercise**

100 things to learn before you're 10

- Throwing ball to wall and catching - this helps to 'get your brain going'..

- Throwing ball to person – or hand to hand - and catching

- **2 minutes - to learn spelling of essential vocabulary (or write out and say a times table – same every day until learnt)**

- Repeatedly copy out 5 words to learn spelling (whether spelling words from school or chosen from First Hundred words)

OR

- Repeatedly copy out and say times table to learn

- **2 minutes - to release tension and develop hand control**

- Squeezing a stress ball or equivalent (plasticine)

- **3 minutes - to mentally prepare for the day**

Look at school timetable. Think through each lesson for the day. Look for when focus will be needed and for about how long. Visualise going through the day (children will need help to do this at the beginning) e.g. to help them get the image, talk about their classroom; their teacher; other children in the class and any of the school routine you know about…

Agree a target for the day..e.g. it might be to concentrate in the first lesson; it might be to be more focused when doing English work that day or to do brilliant handwriting in the first lesson. Choose ONE target that is achievable and that you can ask about after school. This is a development process: it takes time and one target at a time is all that a child can manage, initially!

- **1 minute - to final check preparation**

Help your child to make sure their homework is in the bag and that all that is needed is ready. Have they got their link - if they need one - to help them remember their target? Repeat main focus for today, to make sure the brain has the message.

N.B. All activities need to be timed and STOPPED when the time is up, even if they are not 'finished'. This, with your commentary, will help your child develop concentration. It has been used successfully by many parents to help empower children from as young as 6 years old all the way up to 11 years old, changing the activities appropriately. You can also use this to teach your child to understand deadlines and realise they can speed up if necessary by what they do 'inside themselves'. Timing encourages them to do the activities because they know they have a purpose which is achievable and they are not going to drag on.

It is very important to **confirm** to them - and therefore, to their brain - that improvement is something **they can do** by themselves and if ever they are not sure how to improve they need to ask you, or their teacher.

100 things to learn before you're 10

Lesson 9:
Feelings

> A mother reported on her very bright, 9 year old child's progress. It appeared from what was being said that he was making overall improvement in attitude and behaviour, however, this was inconsistent. He could be organised, systematic and do a great job with his homework and give his mum the impression that he had 'finally' decided to take responsibility for himself; but then, another time she would leave instructions for him to complete work supervised by another adult and she would return to find it not finished.
>
> Understandably, she found this inconsistency frustrating and felt as though they had gone forward three steps and back two. The child, who had overheard what his mum had been saying, was asked why he sometimes didn't do what was asked when it was obvious that he could if he put his mind to it. His response was 'because he 'didn't feel like it'.

From birth to puberty, children are naturally based in feeling. This means that *everything they do* - every 'decision' they make - is based on the **feeling** of what is happening in them and around them. It is unlikely they are generating the feeling themselves, it is more likely to be caused in them as a reaction to what has happened or to what is happening around them in the environment and what they are experiencing. There is no point in asking, 'why did you do that?' because their brain will not have the reference to be able to tell you - whatever they did was a reaction to a feeling they had at that moment. It is an instant reaction, not a thought out response. This is why young children are reactive and spontaneous, rather than responsive.

Bearing this in mind throughout the primary years will help you get to the core when you are trying to interpret your child's behaviour. If your child tells you they 'hate reading', what they mean is that they hate the *feeling* they get when they are reading...if you *change the feeling (perhaps the time of day; the level of book; the person reading)*... so that you change what happens when they read, you will see a big improvement.

Helping children manage feelings - first they need reference:

Everyone has feelings. Feelings are in us when we are born. We have feelings all through our lives. We enjoy positive feelings and smile when we feel good. Feelings are one of the tools we have to tell us what is going on in us and in the world around us. They are there to tell us when we are doing something that is good for us (happy) and when something is not good for us or we are in danger. Feelings are a guide. We have to use other information as well. We cannot rely on feelings because sometimes things happen too fast for them.

Part of the job when we are a child, is to learn to *name, interpret and manage our feelings* so that they do not make us react to things in a way that hurts us or other people.

Managing feelings we call self discipline. Self discipline is an important skill if you want to be an achiever - which is what you have been designed to be. Self discipline means doing what needs to be done, at the time it needs to be done, whether you feel like doing it or not.

Examples can be given here about what mum or dad might feel like doing - but don't!

How to talk to children about negative feelings and how to manage them.

Saying 'don't' to children isn't always enough to stop them developing negative habits or ways of thinking. They need reference first and from the age of 7 years will need a reason to choose to change a way of thinking or a behaviour.

Without a reason, the brain has nothing to 'anchor' the change of behaviour and they will be doing what they are told because they want to please you, copy their friend or because they don't want to get punished. This may bring about a temporary change in behaviour but it is unlikely to last as a positive development.

Choosing to behave a certain way, will help to bring the development of the brain patterns which will ensure that it becomes part of the child's foundation and then it will grow, **because it is what they want**. Reasons help a child to choose and to change. Up to puberty is the time in our lives when it is easiest to change!

Negative feelings that make a human being feel 'bad':

We are not born with any of these negative feelings or behaviours in us. They live in the world and are one of the reactions we can have to things that happen to us in the world.

Negative feelings are there as a guide to tell us something needs to change. It might be that we are doing something which is not good for us and so our body gives us a negative feeling such as uncomfortable, guilty, fed up so that we stop doing it or get what we need.

Or we might get negative feelings as a reaction to something someone else does that doesn't agree with the way we think. Even if we could do it, it is not our job to change another person, we can only change ourselves by changing the way we think or what we do.

Negative feelings are a kind of warning that we need to change or manage something either in ourselves or our environment so that we can stay safe, bright and positive in ourselves.

Remember you can learn to **choose** whether to act on a feeling. It doesn't necessarily matter that you can still feel the feeling because it sometimes takes a little time for your brain to work out what to do with the feeling, but it will work it out. It *does* matter that you learn to manage it so that you can stay bright and happy. Know it, don't act it. Feelings - good and bad - come and go all the time and we do learn to have some control over the way we react.

To help your child learn to manage and respond to feelings positively, it helps to get to the core reason for the negative response so that you are dealing with the cause - the behaviour is a symptom of a difficulty or contradiction at core, it is not 'the child' or their personality.

The most important thing to remember when a child is behaving badly is not to get personally involved! It does not help when an adult gets involved in the feeling that the child has and tries to control it for them! Even when you feel all your buttons are being pushed, stay in control so that you can think! When we lose it, we lose the ability to think as well and can then make rash decisions that we later regret.

Nor does it help to 'ignore' them. If they are having a negative reaction and they know they are not going to get their way - for whatever reason - they need **support** to control the temper or emotion that races through them. Over time, ignoring them can make them feel abandoned just when they need a little support, which can lead to insecurity and self doubt. Standing/sitting with your child or nearby and watching or waiting quietly, gives them reassuring support that shows you know they are grappling with something that - to them - is big and you have every confidence in their ability to do that.

> A seven year old girl came across as very mature, articulate and confident. Parents were at their wits' end, however, because she would refuse to stay in her own bed at night and would go to sleep between them. She would also regularly have tantrums in order to get her own way and in effect, they felt she completely ruled the household and everyone was becoming miserable. None of this was evident in her behaviour at the beginning of the meeting with her. During the parent discussion and feedback that followed, the child appeared in the doorway demanding her father's assistance. When she was calmly told that he was 'busy at the moment' and she would need to wait a few minutes, she immediately stamped her foot, howled and went into a complete meltdown, with huge tears, deep sobs and shaking. This was not an act. This was behaviour that was becoming imbedded and needed help to be managed. Initially, without words, she was calmly taken by the hand, given a tissue and talking kindly at her level, was assured that she was not in trouble; that no one minded what was happening, but no one could talk to her properly while she was in that state and so everyone would wait

100 things to learn before you're 10

> until she calmed herself down. Her brain had been (albeit unintentionally), programmed with this behaviour over several years and so it needed to 'run that program' and test this new response, which meant she continued to cry and howl for another minute or so. Throughout this period of distress, there was a quiet commentary calmly reassuring her and letting her know that no one minded how long it took and that everyone had confidence in her. As she began to get control and calm down, no pressure was put on her to 'hurry up'. Everyone waited until she was feeling much, much better at which point, she was congratulated for taking a big step forward in her self-control and maturity. She was also pleased with herself and smiled, before running off to wash her face. Her mother later said she would never have believed it possible to manage a tantrum that way, if she hadn't witnessed it with her own eyes.

When children are having a negative reaction; management of it can be difficult for parents and equally difficult for the child concerned, who won't necessarily understand why they feel what they feel. They don't need punishment as a first principle, they need help and guidance! Occasionally, a firm reminder of where the boundaries are may be needed, when you know that the child knows better, but up to ten years old, always give the benefit of the doubt first and remain calm in yourself. This will give you time to work out a measured, helpful response rather than a reaction that could make the situation worse. Bear in mind: What is my child *actually* learning from this?

When you meet negativity in your child, the following responses may be helpful in realigning your child to the best of themselves:

- Your behaviour is causing… irritation? frustration? me to feel ignored? (one thing only, please!)… is that what you meant to do?

- Your brain will think that's what you want and make it a habit - is it what you want? If not, change it.

- What are you trying to develop in yourself?

Common negative feelings in children that can trigger a challenging reaction:

It's not fair! - we are born with a sense of justice and fairness. This is totally understood about the natural world. A man-eating lion doesn't mind who he eats! The culture however, is based in gain and loss and competition and is often 'not fair'. The Two Lives and How the Culture Works are a useful tools when explaining this difference to children because one is natural (which they 'get') and one is manmade, which they find contradictory.

Pressure - when we plant a seed in the ground, pressure is the last thing it needs because it will get crushed. In essence, children's development can be thought of the same way. Children will intuitively respond to feelings of pressure by withdrawing or by reacting aggressively.

> The seven year old boy was argumentative about homework. His mother would sit with him each evening after school and try to help him. She was concerned by his poor understanding of maths and was trying to support him with it, having asked the school for extra work to do this. Each evening that they tried to do the work, the boy

> would get angry and upset, and after a while, so would the mother. No progress was being made.
>
> To resolve this situation, it was suggested that the mother sit with her son as normal to do the homework, but that she was to say nothing. Not a word. Not even, 'would you like a drink or have you got a pencil?' The suggestion was that she simply watch as a witness to what he did and not say anything at all, unless he asked for help of some kind which she could give as briefly as possible.
>
> This was illuminating for both. *He* discovered that he could do more than he thought and his confidence began to grow. *She* discovered that he could do more than she thought, but that he needed more time to get there. Both, in different ways, realised the tension caused by mother's concern that was interpreted as criticism by the child, had created pressure. Maths was the link that sent them into the habitual behaviour which then created more pressure.

When you are creating a neural pathway, pressure is the last thing you need. Imagine learning to drive or learning to play the piano under pressure! We go….slowly, slowly, slowly…while the pathways are created and the skills developed. Once you have made and developed those neural pathways then the pressure can come from **inside you** to run them.

Pressure from outside stops the neural pathways we want from being created and can be the cause of much distress, underachievement and underperformance.

Sarcasm - young children don't understand this, but they feel the negativity of it. Avoid sarcasm if possible because it causes confusion and contradiction in them which makes them feel insecure and robs them of confidence - especially if adults around are laughing at a 'joke' they don't understand. If you can't avoid it, then at least explain it so that your child's brain can recognise it and manage it on future occasions.

Worry - doesn't really help us, it uses energy and doesn't get a result, BUT, we do it! Brains will sometimes go on worrying out of habit even when *you* don't want to, so it is helpful to teach children to learn to manage it by giving themselves a time to worry.

For example say to your child: train yourself to worry at a given time and don't allow yourself to spend time on it even if the thought comes through your mind outside of that time, just dismiss it. Carry on as though it isn't there, until the time you have set to deal with it. So, decide a time that works for you - e.g. 6 o'clock - and say you will give yourself 5 whole minutes to worry as much as you want. Believe it or not, it's extremely difficult to worry deliberately for five whole minutes, but persevere, this is a management strategy so that worry does not get in your way! Have a piece of paper and something to write with and write it all down if that helps during the 'worry time' and then destroy the paper as a symbolic way of showing your brain you don't want that worry.

At the end of the five minutes, you have to stop and set another worry time, for the same worry or any other worry that comes up in the meantime.

Time it precisely and tell your brain you don't want to worry at the end of that time. If you need to, set aside a minute or so each day and put the worry in there. It is possible to train yourself to manage worry in this way if it is not possible to change the situation to stop the worry.

There are also a number of resources that can help you teach children how to distance themselves from worry or find a way to manage it, such as the Guatemalan worry dolls (or you can make your own from matchsticks); or the Worry Eater to name a couple. Books such as Silly Billy by Anthony Brown or The Huge Bag of Worries by Virginia Ironside are both excellent for starting a discussion about worry with young children.

Poem:
The oldest in his family

The oldest in his family
And yet still very young,
I met a boy not long ago
Who was feeling rather glum

He thought that he was 'stupid',
He was timid and withdrawn,
It didn't matter what he did
He was always somehow 'wrong'.

For years he had been watching
All the others in his class
And thinking they were clever
His feelings would not pass.

And then one day it dawned on him
The realisation clear -
Between him and the oldest
There was a whole, full *year*!

He cast aside his doubt and gloom
He was no longer 'slow'
He worked so hard within six months
Results began to show!

His parents loved him dearly,
His classmates loved him too -
But till he loved himself as well,
Then nothing really grew.

So please take care with every child
And do not call them 'slow'
Hurt feelings dampen spirit
And affect how they then grow.

100 things to learn before you're 10

Lesson 10:
Boundaries, Consequences and Taking Responsibility

It helps children when they understand there are actually two sets of rules in the world. It is recommended you refer to this fact often throughout the primary years and it may be included when you talk about the Two Lives. Reference is made to this in other sections of the book as well.

The Two Sets of Rules we inherited at birth:

Natural - inflexible, fixed, core natural boundaries

- These are automatic and to do with 'how things work'.

- They are not personal.

- If you jump off a building you will go down just like anyone else.

- You will burn if you sit in the sun too long.

- There aren't too many natural rules.

- Instinct often helps with them - we get a feeling we are not doing the right thing.

- They are created to help with development, growth and evolution.

- Everyone all around the world has to live by them.

- You can rely on them.

Man made - flexible, not fixed

- These are rules made by people to help everyone live together comfortably in their culture.

- They are often made from what people like or don't like.

- Your parents will try to teach you the ones that you need to know before you are 5 years old, so that you can be sure of yourself when you are at school or in your friend's house.

- The rules in your house might be different to the ones in your friend's house.

- It is best to check.

- Because these rules are made by people, there are sometimes differences between what people think is right or not right and this can cause opinion and argument.

This is what 'boundaries' can be like for children. They are born aligned to natural order and rules and without reference to the culture, they cannot fail to be confused by human behaviour which conflicts with natural order. When there is contradiction between what you say and what you do, children will always react to how it makes them feel, because they are based at the core. Until they have cultural reference, they may **feel** confused, unsure or unsafe. To help them, they need to know the expectation and behaviour so they can work out what they need to do and why.

Example: it is important to have good manners (a 'cultural' rule) because that shows you care about how other people feel and that you want to give a good impression of yourself (a core reason).

Children also need to know that you mean what you say. Repeating yourself over and over saying, 'I mean it, just you wait and see'…even little and often, tells their brain - and yours - that either you do not have a consequence or you do not mean what you say, either way, the brain interprets this as 'there is no need to listen'. It's how it works. It is not personal.

Where there are no fixed boundaries - ones that children *must* respect - they do not feel safe and will always 'play up', 'be naughty', 'push the boundaries' to let you know that something needs to happen, to let you know that they are feeling insecure until the boundaries are fixed. This is a child's natural response to an unknown environment (the world).

It helps children to know that the reason we have boundaries is to keep them safe in the world while they develop self discipline and learn to control and manage themselves.

Consequences - keeping them simple and effective

- If you stand out in the rain, you will get wet

- If you jump off something high, you will go down

- If you uproot a tree, it will die

These are actions with consequences that are easy to see and remember. The consequence is a natural follow up to the action. They are impersonal.

To prevent contradiction, this needs to be true of the consequences we create for the children, too.

Here are a couple of **examples** of simple and effective consequences which will help your child to understand what their actions cause and help you to teach them to take responsibility:

- If you don't do your homework, you will need to go to school and explain to your teacher why it wasn't done…(rather than, 'you won't get pudding', which has nothing to do with homework!)

- If you hurt your brother or sister, you will need to apologise and do two kind things for them to balance it…(rather than, 'you'll lose your pocket money', unless, of course, you are paying them to be nice to their siblings!)

Managing a Tantrum

When children are learning to control powerful emotions like frustration or anger, they may swear at you, hit you, stamp their feet. This will be the manufactured energy being used up - it has to go somewhere and until they develop the skill to use or diffuse it safely; they need your help.

1. Do not take it personally. This is the reaction any child could have to a build up of frustration.

2. Stay calm even though you may be bursting to take control - if you try to take over, the child won't learn to take control and the situation can be inflamed and get worse.

3. If you think they don't already know the behaviour is unacceptable; point this out 'You are not allowed to swear at me/hit me/behave like that *no matter what has happened*'….they do not need a lecture at this point!

4. If this is not the first time and you know *they* know the behaviour is unacceptable. SAY NOTHING! THEY KNOW! They are still learning to control the powerful emotion. This is something even adults can find difficult, so give your child time to develop this without punishment.

5. Remember your child is learning to control something very powerful. This will take all their concentration and energy and if you start shouting or lecturing them, it adds to what they are trying to manage and slows down the recovery!

6. If necessary, make sure neither of you can be physically hurt. Hold their wrist if they are lashing out and keep back from flailing legs. It won't be for long; a huge outburst of emotion is extremely draining for anyone and the energy is soon used up.

7. When your child has calmed themselves down; suggest to them that they go to wash their face, or you do it for them (the face is where the heat and static electricity build up in an energetic explosion and why they go so red in the face. Cool water helps to rebalance the system)

8. Once they are calm and in recovery, give them some reflection and confirm for them if it was quicker or more controlled than previously - this lets their brain know that they are going in the right direction. When you are ready, tell them what was well done or advise them for if/when it happens again.

   e.g. words to the effect of:

   I could see it was a struggle but that didn't take so long that time, well done - you're beginning to get more self control.

   The following reflections can be helpful in bringing the child back to the best of themselves:

   It hurts when you hit me. I'm just like you and don't like being hurt. It upsets me a lot, because you are better than that.

   What are you trying to grow in yourself?

When you do that, it causes ……..Is that what you wanted me to think?

Speaking like this, gives responsibility to your child but it also gives them guidance and reassurance.

9. If they have calmed down, children will be very quick to apologise and want to make it better. They live in the moment and don't bear grudges. If they cannot 'feel it'; to them, it isn't there any more.

Aggressive behaviour in young children is normally a struggle to interpret and manage emotions. In older children (10+) aggressive behaviour can be calculated and deliberate because they have not learnt to take responsibility and the brain is exerting itself as dominant. This needs different management to re-educate, 're-wire' (which means, make a different pathway in the brain) and re-train the brain so that they learn to take responsibility. This book is focused on creating a strong foundation from the start.

Poem:
Setting Boundaries

Early in September
The first day of the term
I waited in my classroom
for the children to return

I stood and watched in horror
As they came tumbling in
Pushing, shoving, fighting
They were making quite a din

I waited very calmly
And didn't say a word
There wasn't really any point
I wouldn't have been heard

After fully fifteen minutes
When all had settled down
They noticed I was standing there
Arms folded, looking round

'I am amazed you did that
Rushing in without a care,
No one said, 'Good morning, Miss'
T'was as if I wasn't there

This is the start of your last year
The start of future's bright
I would have thought you'd take some time
To try to get it right

I spoke to them quite softly
I didn't scream and shout
I wanted them to get the point
They turned and looked about

I'm sure you must have manners
But I cannot see quite where
Please use them when you're with me
I've got mine and so that's fair.'

The room was full of silence
The lesson went home well
They got the point quite clearly
The next day, I could tell.

Begin at the beginning
The first moment starts the day
And what you do within it
Sets the standard and the way.

Lesson 11:
Comprehension

> When asked what he thought comprehension was, the 10 year old boy said, 'it's when you're given something to read and then you have to answer questions on it'.

The majority of children have given, in essence, the same answer when asked what they understand by comprehension. This is to do with their reference and experience of 'comprehension', which is something they see they 'do at school' rather than a number of thinking processes that are developed and applied in life.

To engage the children in developing their thinking processes and boosting their confidence and achievement, it helps to define comprehension in its broadest sense. If you give your child the following example they will get a 'feel' for comprehension and a better understanding of what it involves. Say to them that if they saw you come in the house, dripping wet, holding a brolly and stamping your boots, they would be able to work out what the weather was doing, even if they hadn't looked out of the window. Ask them to make sure!

When they tell you it means it is raining, explain that what they have done in their heads to reach that conclusion is what comprehension really means - i.e. being able to put together information from 'outside' of themselves, whether it is something read, seen, heard, smelled or touched, and connecting it with stuff they already know stored in their experience so that they understand what the information is telling them.

When it comes to reading, many children become 'free readers' as soon as they are able to decode all the words in their reading book. However, a great many children are able to read all the words without being able to understand the meaning simply because they lack reference and experience. Look at the following passage which is the first paragraph from an 11+ English comprehension paper:

The building is enormous. Whenever we're there it's almost empty, because it's Saturday; this makes it seem even larger.

It's of dark brown weathered brick, and gives the impression of having turrets, although it has none. Ivy grows on it, leafless now in winter, covering it with skeletal veining. Inside it there are long hallways with hardwood floors, stained and worn from generations of students in slushy winter boots, but still kept polished.

Now look at the passage again with notes about the reference needed to really understand it.

The building is enormous. (Knowledge of size - what is 'enormous'? Bigger than school? Smaller? ...)

Whenever we're there it's almost empty, because it's Saturday; (you need to understand that people don't work in this building on Saturday because it is the weekend. Often parents DO work at the weekend, so some children may not understand this sentence because they have not learned to infer or because they do not have the reference needed to do that.)

this makes it seem even larger. (you need to have the comparison of a space with and without people or things to know **why** it 'seems larger')

It's of dark brown weathered brick, (you need to understand the meaning of 'weathered' and what happens to brick in this context for the brain to create the image) *and gives the impression of having turrets,* (you need to know what turrets are and where they are usually found) *although it has none.* (This is confusing and needs to be discussed for the child to understand how it is possible it 'gives the impression' of having turrets, but doesn't actually have them) *Ivy grows on it,* (you need to know what ivy is and how it grows. Many children may not have seen ivy growing and wouldn't know what the building looks like.) *leafless now in winter,* (if you don't have the reference for ivy, you will not understand why it is 'leafless in winter') *covering it with skeletal veining* (to understand and get an image of this, you need to be able to define 'skeletal' as being to do with skeleton and veining to do with the way the leaf works and decays. After that your brain needs to put together an image of how the building looks and why it is relevant to the setting) *Inside it there are long hallways with hardwood floors,* (not many, if any, children will understand what a 'hardwood floor' means nor that it indicates the age of the building *stained and worn from generations of students* ('stained'... 'generations of students' needs definition to be understood) *in slushy winter boots, but still kept polished.*

Your child may be very bright but when it comes to comprehension, if they don't have the reference or experience, their brain will not be able to make the connections or form the images in their minds for them to understand the text. It would be like trying to make omelettes when you haven't got eggs. Can't be done. It is very common to find children 'reading' without being able to interpret or understand all the way up to and beyond, 14 years of age!

While your children are young, gathering reference and building neural pathways in earnest, you can help by setting aside 10 minutes (timed) at least three times a week for 9-11 year old and more, preferably daily, if younger, to really listen to your child read and provide the reference, check the comprehension, even if only a paragraph, certainly until they leave Year 6. If a child reads 'ivy', they need to be able to visualise and connect it in their brain; searching Google on your phone for an image of 'ivy' is better than nothing, but going out in the garden or park, finding ivy in its environment and looking at it in all its glory will mean they get the experience of ivy which is much more beneficial. If 'a picture is worth a thousand words', then the real experience must be worth ten thousand times as much!

A brain cannot learn to visualise unless it has visual references. It affects maths too…

> A child of about 7 or 8 was stuck on a maths problem to do with the price of sausages. Even after reading the problem out aloud, she didn't know quite what to do, until she was asked if she had ever been in the butchers in the High Street. Her response was immediate, 'ohhhh, I get it!'. Her brain made the association with the problem and was able to visualise and solve it.

You have no idea what an elephant is really like just by looking at a picture or 'imagining' - how do you do that if you've never seen one?! The 'experience of elephant' is very different because you get to feel the presence of elephant, hear the sound of elephant, smell the smell of elephant (you need it all for the full experience!) and *you cannot get these online, on tv or in books*. You have to actually go and SEE an elephant to fully comprehend it!

The key is QUALITY not quantity. One paragraph really listened to is so much better than 4 pages half listened to while you cook and try to control two other smaller, distracting children! It is understood that when they read 'for pleasure' it is absolutely fine for children to just 'get the gist' of what they are reading, but this does not develop reading or thinking skills as effectively nor as quickly as an in-depth burst of comprehension, adult reflection, commentary and reference gathering, even if it is for 'just' ten minutes.

Lesson 12:
What Children need to know about School

It is a sad fact that if you were to pop your head into many primary classrooms in this country, no matter how hard the teacher is working, you would undoubtedly spot many little faces looking and behaving at times as though school is being 'done' to them. In effect, unless the child has worked out **very good reason** personally for being there which **fully engages** them - apart from 'my parents make me go', then they are correct! This can mean success in learning can rely heavily on the personality and skill of the teacher and the relationship the child has with them, rather than on an established and purposeful firm foundation.

When asked if they would still go to school if their parents said it was ok not to, the majority of children said they would. When asked why, some said they wanted to see their friends, some said they liked the lunch, some said they enjoy playtime and a few, said they wanted to learn, but couldn't specify exactly what they want to learn.

The first thing children need to see is the bigger picture and where school fits in life, with reference to the Two Lives. They need to review what is happening and see that between birth and 5, they are largely with their parents or carers, who teach them basic things which encourage independence.

For an effective way to go through this, it is helpful to have a piece of paper and a pencil. Sit beside your child. Draw a line across the page, put 0 at one end and 100 at the other and tell your child: *this is the line of life.*

0......10......20......30......40......50......60......70......80......90.....100

Continue:

When you were born, you knew nothing.
You didn't know what day it was or where you were.

You didn't even know what your name was!

The only things you could do were move, sleep, eat, cry and make noise *(and anything else you or your child can add!) This brief summary of how they were when they were born causes the brain to reflect and think about what has happened so far in life.* The first five years *(mark it on the line)*, you spent mostly with….*(parents/carers?)*..who taught you: *(make a list with your child of what they learned before 5 - examples follow):*

- to speak

- to recognise things - by 5yrs you can fairly safely point to just about anything in the house and the child will be able to name it - this fact needs to be pointed out to them! It's actually quite a feat when you think about it!

- to walk

- to wash

- to brush teeth

- to tidy

Make a full list - it's important because it reinforces to their brain how much they have learnt and how far they have come.

When you feel you have done that, tell them that: 'at 5yrs old, it is the law in this country that all children should go to school so that they can learn what they need to know about how the world works so that they can be independent, look after themselves and understand the way things work here.'

Draw lines that mark 5-16 years old:

0……10……20……30……40……50……60……70……80……90…..100

and explain that 'this is how much time in your whole life that you go to school'.

'First you go to infant/primary school, then onto secondary/high school. At the end of that you may leave or go on to college and university, both of which may be important in preparing you for the rest of your world life.'

It needs to be stressed, however, because children **do not know** that: *'you are not there to become something school wants. You are there to use school to develop yourself and your skills so you need to make as much use of it as possible'*.

Children who have been withdrawn in class or described as shy have found it helpful to be told one or more of the following:

When you are in the classroom, imagine it is just you and your teacher and so if they ask a question, try to answer it…and if you are confused or not sure what to do, ask them.

It is the teacher's job to teach and it is your job to learn. The teacher has instructions about what children need to learn and that is their job. If you are finding it hard or you don't understand, it is your job to let the teacher know. The teacher does not know what is going on in your head unless you tell them but if you feel shy or don't want to do that in front of everybody; just ask the teacher at break time or when everyone else is getting on quietly with their work. If you still feel uncomfortable about it, then see if mum can help….

Describe the development benefits as you see them from what your child is doing at school: here are some examples:

Maths helps to train your brain to think in organised ways; it helps your brain to understand order, processes and systems and you need to be able to do these things when you are working in the world.

English helps you to develop your language and communication skills so that you can get along with people. There are a huge number of people in the world now and it really helps if you can learn to get along and express yourself, so this is part of what you are trying to develop in school.

Being in a classroom with other children helps you to develop patience, because you cannot always be seen immediately; you can develop your concentration, organisation and listening skills as well. There isn't a magic wand that taps you on the head when you are 18 years old to let you know that you are an adult, you need to develop the skills and abilities that are going to work for you in this life and the best time to start is while you are young.

Talking to your children in this way makes more sense of school to them and helps them understand the different reasons for the actions that you ask them to make. The brain loves to think in development terms. School becomes a place of growth and achievement (which will not necessarily be a tick on a page) and ANY schoolwork can be used to develop some aspect of their human core. This is examined more closely in the section on Homework.

Lesson 13:
Organisation and Planning

> As the 12 year old boy prepared for school entrance exams, he found that although he knew how to answer the questions and how to do the papers required, he could never seem to finish in the time allowed. This was causing him - and his parents and teachers - anxiety. This is not at all uncommon when children have not fully grasped the concept of time or been taught how to plan and use time efficiently. It's a skill that needs to be learned.

As children get older (key stage 2 and onwards) those who have poor organisation skills will be found to have one or more of the following indicators:

- Untidy handwriting

- Messy books

- Unfinished work

- Forgotten homework

- Poor concentration

- Poor comprehension

- Exam results that do not reflect ability

- Apathy

- Poor motivation

- Frustration

- Avoidance tactics

- Negative attitude towards self and work

- Poor memory

- Low self esteem

The list could continue...and lead to your child feeling stressed and overwhelmed by the time they reach secondary school. However, you can help to prevent your child developing these characteristics by teaching them how to organise and plan rather than leaving it to chance.

Being Organised helps the brain:

- Prioritise (an important skill)

- Appreciate value

- Make connections faster (it is systematic in storing reference)

- Store the Systems you create so that when you have a task to do you can think of a way to do it (helpful for children in exams and then in life)

- Become methodical

- Improve attention to detail

- Encourage the development of care (a natural essence to grow)

Here is an exercise to teach children about organisation: you can use this exercise with children from the age of 7 years...

You need: a collection of about 30-40 small objects which are different sizes, different colours and different shapes. You can use any of the following:

> counters or
> building blocks or
> buttons or
> beads or
> items from you kitchen - anything you can form into a group on a table top.

Show your child all the objects and ask them to sort them. If they ask, 'how', simply repeat the instruction with a smile and a nod and watch what they do, without further pressure or interruption.

When they have finished sorting, ask them what criteria they used. Explain criteria as the reason they used to put the objects into groups. They may say, 'colour' or 'shape' or whatever criteria they used. Don't judge or criticise their reasons. Their brain will be sorting against the criteria it knows and this exercise is going to help your child begin to think outside their own 'box' by linking things together in different ways - this is what learning is all about.

Ask your child if there is another way to sort the objects. Let them think about this and they will soon begin to reorganise against a different criterion. Again, when the objects have been rearranged, ask what criteria was used and ask if there is another, different way to reorganise the objects.

Using a set of foam shapes in three colours, different children consistently found at least 5 different ways to rearrange the groups - by colour; shape; size; thickness; number of sides....and more. Let your child work to find as many different ways to sort your objects as they can. Be encouraging and confirming of what they do. They might surprise you with their ingenuity! To begin with, resist the temptation to make suggestions to give their brain time to gather information from their experience.

When you feel you have exhausted the different sorting criteria, talk to your child about the fact that there is often more than one way to organise things. Some things are organised for us - like the dictionary which is always in alphabetical order; a system which, once learned, is easy for all of us to use. However, each of our lives is different and we can choose how we organise things to suit what we are trying to do.

Talk to them about how being organised keeps the house clean; helps the kitchen work efficiently; talk to them about your criteria for your own organisation, especially where it has a direct affect on them.

Work with your child to think about what we organise and why, such as:

- Our things - so that we can find what we need and take good care of them

- Our routines - so that we don't waste energy working out what to do

- Our work - so that we get the job done

- Our time - so that we don't waste time and achieve our goals

- Our diet and nutrition - so we stay healthy

- Our day - so that we make sure to do what needs to be done and rest

- Our homes - so that everyone is comfortable…

This exercise is a good way of opening discussion about how your child's room is organised (or not!) and what affect that has on their brain. Children do not know unless it is made conscious in them, that it is more difficult to think in a messy environment because there are too many conflicting distractions grabbing the attention of their brain. If their room is very messy or things are in a muddle, how might they fix it so that their brain is satisfied? The brain works better in an organised space. Having said this, they need to know that during a creative process, the space can become very *dis*organised in the enthusiasm of invention but at some point, the 'resting' point for the brain will be organised. This will encourage them to develop good habits which will help in their lives.

Confirm for your child that we work internally according to a series of systems e.g. the digestive system; the respiratory system; the system of muscles and so on and they all work together to keep us well. To keep stress to a minimum, we work best when we develop systems that work for us in our world life, too. One of the ways we can do this is through planning.

Planning

In a similar way to Organisation, children who do not learn to plan are likely to:

- Underperform at school - because their thinking patterns are not as developed as they could be by practising the process of planning

- Resist homework - because *they* were 'planning' to do something else after school...and homework does not take priority

- Fall below anticipated levels of achievement - because they prioritise against a different set of criteria to you

- Be more easily overwhelmed by increasing amounts of homework as it appears in their life (especially when they reach high/secondary school)

- Lack self discipline - because there is no structure in place

- Have a negative attitude to work - because it impinges on what they see as 'free time' and if they don't get satisfaction from it, they naturally feel resentful

Planning is a process which takes time to learn. What children need to help them learn to plan:

- An understanding of the World Life/Natural Life and how they work together

- An appreciation of time;

- An understanding of their growing responsibilities

- An understanding of the reasons why they need to do some things even though they would prefer to do others;

- An ability to prioritise and

- They need to develop flexibility and the ability to compromise at times.

Reference to give an appreciation of time - the foundation for planning

The following list of 60 activities can be used to give the brain the experience of doing something for 1, 2 or 3 minutes. When you time these activities precisely you help your child consolidate the concept of time which is essential for them to be able to estimate how long a piece of work or an activity is likely to take them. **Always use a large timer they can see while they do these activities.** You will need to help by: giving the instruction; timing precisely; witnessing and confirming what happens (no criticism!); congratulating at the end.

Children of 5-6 years need to become familiarised with ONE MINUTE so keep the activities to one minute for them. Children from 7 years onwards (even up to 11 years), need to learn to be able to make different kinds of calculations about time and how much time they need or have got for various activities. To develop this area, use these activities for up to 3 minutes. By repeating the same activity several times while encouraging the child to improve, you can help them develop not just a sense of time but also the skill or quality written beside them. **You need to tell your child what they are focusing on** if you want them the brain to register it as reference.

1. Count - or write - things beginning with b - observation

2. Be silent for one minute – self control

3. Keep still for one whole minute (or more) – self control

4. Balance on one leg for one minute – self control

5. Write the letter 'a' improving each time for a minute – self control, presentation skills, build stamina or determination

6. Learn a word in one minute – improve vocabulary, practise writing, exercise memory strategies

7. Identify sounds you can hear in one minute – build confidence

8. Say a times table over and over for one minute – brain training

9. Do a one minute tidy up – observation, sensitivity, encourage value and care

10. Tap a rhythm for a minute – follow instruction and coordinate

11. Slow motion for one minute – self control, self knowledge

12. Carry a glass full of water without spilling any for a minute – self control, concentration

13. Describe an object – support versatility, vocabulary and creativity

14. Keep eyes closed for one minute – self-control and listening to self

15. Balance a book on your head – self control and focus

16. Say 20 things you could use a paperclip for – promote creativity and ingenuity

17. Count in 2's to 100 – brain training

18. Count in 5's to 150 – brain training

19. Count in 10's to 500 – brain training

20. Choose a word in the dictionary and see what it means – improve range of vocabulary and versatility

21. Write down as many adjectives as you can (begin with a certain letter) think of – brain exercise

22. Hit a target – hand/eye coordination

23. Click your fingers – body control

24. Walk on toes – body training

25. Walk on heels – stimulates brain

26. Hum – evens out emotion

27. Whistle – evens out emotion

28. Shout – great for knowing how loud you CAN be

29. Listen – long range – learn to extend focus

100 things to learn before you're 10

30. Listen – short range – learn to direct focus

31. Whisper – body control

32. Watch – outside your window – improve observation

33. Look at the sky – improve observation

34. Smell all the herbs in the kitchen – build reference

35. Read a cereal packet – make conscious the unconscious

36. Count the contents of my purse – knowledge about sequencing and ordering

37. Follow the leader – follow instructions

38. Touch and compare the feeling of as many different surfaces as possible – gather reference

39. Cut out a shape with left hand – fine motor skills

40. Cut out a shape with right hand – fine motor skills

41. Draw – develop artistic skills and appreciation

42. Name all the things your hands do for you and be grateful – develop self care and appreciation

43. Mirroring exercise – develop observation and work as a team

44. Dance for a minute – control and rhythm

45. Name things that come in two's – develop reference

46. Learn to tie a knot – gather reference

47. Learn to tie a bow – gather reference

48. Find as many green things as possible in time given – choosing and gathering

49. Organise homework area – organisation skills

50. Name as many plants as possible in a minute – reference

51. Wiggle toes for one minute – body feeling and control

52. Walk on the spot for one minute – even out feelings

53. Shake your body for one minute – body awareness/feelings

54. Arm wrestle for one minute – know limitations

55. Play pat-a-cake – memory and concentration exercise

56. Hula hoop for one minute – develop confidence, body knowledge and awareness

57. Play the card game Blink (or similar) – speed of process

58. Knead playdough for one minute – strengthen muscles

59. Practise folding paper – precision and care training

60. Do spot-the-difference – observation

Setting Targets with your child

Teaching your child to plan will take more than one conversation! Keep it simple. One step at a time. Start with small targets that they can achieve e.g:

Packing school bag and ask you to check (initially)

Plan homework

Look at the timetable at the needs of the next day so that you can arrive with everything you need.

Homework is a great way to develop the ability to set targets. Your child will need help at first.

Begin early with 5 year olds 'planning' birthday parties, Christmas or other family events with you

Move onto planning trips with them.

By age 8-9 years you can introduce the idea of taking more responsibility for planning their homework (do it together).

By age 9-11 years the children need to be able to plan work and organise their thinking to make best use of their energy.

Important Points to get across to your child about the Advantages of Planning and why they need to learn to do it:

- you feel in control of your work

- your brain gets ready for what you have planned and creates the energy needed for you to do it

- you enjoy your free time more because you don't need to worry about work

- you have better focus because your brain knows what it needs to do

- you do what needs to be done

- you can balance work and pleasure (which is very important)

- there is less stress

- you feel more responsible and get a sense of satisfaction

- you develop skills that will be important in your working life

- you are less vulnerable to being overwhelmed by stress in adulthood.

Children of 10+ years can be given the following guidance.

Planning for Success - when you are in an exam year

1. What do you need to achieve?

2. How much time have you got before you need to achieve it?

3. What is happening during this time?

    It helps the brain get 'the bigger picture' by having a blank calendar to write on, in front of them.

    Make a note of all the events that need to be on your plan: Holidays, Christmas, Birthdays (discuss with parents as well). These will be occasions when you do not want to work (and nor should you need to if you plan properly!)

4. Work out how much study time is left after all commitments have been recorded on the plan.

BE REALISTIC!! Take account of school and homework, which obviously come first and then put in revision periods.

If possible, include one day off from study each week - your brain needs to rest as well as work hard. This is especially important in the weeks before exams.

'Work hard/Play hard'! Scheduled rest needs to be timed and allowed without interruption or discussion of work or the brain complains! 'Rest' in this case does not include the night's sleep, which should also be on the plan. The brain needs to see graphically, that work does not overpower the schedule. One way to do this, is to use one colour for 'work' (which includes time at school) and one colour for 'not work/rest/playdates'. By colouring the schedule in this way you are showing your child - who may *feel* that it's 'all work' - that actually, work is not dominating their day.

Re-visit the section on Time and go through the 24 hour day highlighting work periods in the colour you have chosen as part of showing your child how to plan for themselves. Children love it when they can act independently; teaching them to plan is a big part of the process.

100 things to learn before you're 10

Lesson 14:
Homework

> During a pleasant summer holiday, the family were kept waiting for four hours while their 9 year old held them to ransom over a piece of unfinished work. In the end their trip was cancelled and what had promised to be an enjoyable family outing turned into a disappointing, lacklustre day for all.

There are many reasons for the battles that are fought over homework in homes throughout the land. Here is a list of the most common ones. It is not exhaustive!

- Something that would take 30 minutes in school, can actually turn into a two hour battle at home. This is because the environment at home is completely different. The expectations are different. The organisation is different. The priorities are different. Not better. Not worse. Different.

- Children forget their homework and leave it at school. This is usually to do with poor organisation skills, lack of responsibility and low expectations.

- Children don't remember what to do. It was 10 a.m. when the homework was issued. They live in the moment. It's almost dinner time. 10 a.m. was years ago.

- The child cannot read the instructions - and if they can, they can't understand them or work out what to do because the language is formal and their comprehension hasn't developed to that level.

- Children don't see the purpose of the homework (and let's face it, sometimes, neither do you).

- Too much is happening at the same time as the child is trying to do their homework:

- There is too much noise

- The TV and technology beckon

- No-one is listening

- The child needs a pencil sharpener…eraser…..ruler….

- No-one is setting the pace

- Dinner smells nice - brains are easily distracted by the simplest of things!

- The telephone rings and distracts you

- They need the loo

- There are no meaningful consequences to the homework not being done

- Bribery has been used too often

- There are siblings causing a disturbance

- There are too many interruptions

- There is no routine

- There is no end…….for anyone…….!

For homework to be successful and meaningful your child needs:

Structure - choose a convenient time of day and stick to it. It doesn't need to be the same time every day; but it needs to be routine. In other words, it could be 5-6pm on Monday every Monday, 4-5pm on Wednesday and every Wednesday, after tea on Friday and so on. Pin it up somewhere everyone can see it. This is really important for your child's brain. When they understand ahead of time what the expectation is, then there is less resistance and argument.

A definite 'homework is done here' space. Up to 7 or 8 years old, children don't like to be left alone to work; you need to keep them company even if they are working independently. Ideally, you need to be focused on them. This is to reassure their brain that what they are doing is correct. Remember we are aiming to use homework for development reasons so they will rely on you to give feedback at some point on what they are doing.

Support - get them going by reading through the homework with them and making sure they know what to do. It is not always practical to keep your children company for the whole time while they do homework, organise a few minutes one-to-one help and **time** it. It will be of enormous benefit to your child and the atmosphere around homework! Tell your child words to the effect of: *'I can give you 5 minutes, then I'm going to get on with cooking for 10 minutes then I will come back for another X minutes. You can ask me questions if you need to while I'm cooking. I'll be as quiet as I can while you're working and don't worry about interrupting me because I'm here to help.'*

Resources - a fairly comprehensive list follows. Put them into a box ready and keep them in a known place. Anything borrowed from the box must be returned straight away after use so there is no disturbance to the homework routine and no excuse for wandering around 'looking' for things.

A purpose* - are they trying to improve a skill such as presentation? Or develop creativity? Or are they trying to learn new content (like times tables, spellings or history facts?). Each homework session needs a specific purpose and **ONE measurable target** so your child can see when they have achieved it and hearty congratulations can be given. More is written about this below.

A timer - homework should ALWAYS have a time limit! Lessons in school don't go on forever if you don't finish by break. You still need to go to your next lesson. Homework should be given the same expectation or the brain will not learn to focus and deliver in the time given. Developing this is crucial not only for sitting exams, which every child needs to do at some point, whether we like it or not but essentially in their future working life as well.

Consequences - if homework is not done in the agreed time, you will already have alerted your child's teacher, that they will return to school with it and explain what happened. Your child's teacher will be aware that you are focused on developing their independence and responsibility and will know that you give your support for them to make sure it is finished in their break time, to reinforce the fact that there are consequences. If, of course, the homework is too difficult, the teacher will need to know so they can go over it again.

Here's a simple way to remember what you need for HOMEWORK:

- **H** ave a timetable and clock/timer available

- **O** rganise things needed - from a ready prepared kit

- **M** ake sure task is understood - read it to them

- **E** nsure environment is clear of distraction

- **W** ork out a specific target for the session

- **O** ffer commentary, guidance and reflection as needed

- **R** ead instructions carefully

- **K** eep focused until finished then reward (with praise, positive feedback, a game...) and relax!

A Purpose*: Using Homework for Personal Development (and still giving the teacher what they want).

We know from the learning process that 'going through the motions' with any activity, doesn't achieve anything meaningful in terms of development. If your child is not engaged with an activity, it can even be counter productive, causing a negative attitude; apathy or argument whenever they are asked to do anything, which will be frustrating for you and for them. To avoid this situation, here are some ways to use homework so that it is a positive experience that will encourage your children's development and give you, their parent, more tools and focus for supporting their education.

Spelling words are often sent home from school weekly to be learned for a test the following week. The children are usually expected to write them out each evening and also write a sentence containing each word. The great thing is: this is a routine. The not so great thing is: it can be very boring! If your child brings home spellings to learn every week, it is because that is the way the school have chosen to teach them. Don't fight it. Don't let it get boring either. Liven it up! Use the exercise for personal development.

Some suggestions of how you might do this follow: the important thing to remember is that you must **focus only on one thing at a time** otherwise the brain cannot master it! Neuroscientists now have proof that the brain cannot multi task. It can change quickly between tasks, but it does not multi task, especially while it is developing. Instructions often tell children to, 'Look in the dictionary for the words you don't know, write interesting sentences in your best handwriting and do it in half an hour'. To do 'interesting' sentences they need to have access to plenty of experience and reference; to look in a dictionary for a word they don't know takes some children up to 10 minutes because it is a huge book and they only learned alphabetical order six months before; to do 'best handwriting' is a whole bunch of skills to accomplish properly and coordinating all that in half an hour is a bit of a tall order for a developing brain at the end of long day at school. Keep in mind : your child is trying to gather reference, make connections, grow neural pathways and cover them with myelin. This takes time, care, patience, support, focus and practise. Lots of practise!

Although the following ideas are presented as 'Week 1, Week 2' and so on, you can use the ideas in any order and for as long as it takes for the target to be achieved. You may decide to change the focus every week or to focus on one thing for six weeks or a term until it is achieved, but the examples here are suggestions for you to use and adapt for your own child. In the process of building the skill, they will be learning and becoming familiar with the spelling words; homework will be more interesting; your child will feel more positive and that you are supporting them. Always let your child know what skill you/they are focusing on and if they start to tell you there is something specific *they* would like to improve - go with that!

Week 1: Tell your child that this week you're going to use the spelling homework to **develop memory skills:** Write each spelling word on two cards and play 'Pairs'. (Spread them out face down on the table and take turns to turn over two cards. If they match you get to keep them, if not, you turn them back over and the other person has a go). If you do this, the focus is on memory which means *you* need to make suggestions for the sentences to be written for the teacher. Your child will be learning the words through the memory game. They do not need the added stress of thinking up sentences as well, especially if they are unfamiliar words. They need to gather reference for those words. You have that reference! You can brainstorm them together and then record them on a phone for your child to write them down to take back to school.

Week 2: Tell them they're going to focus on **developing self discipline** this week. Give your child the definition: self discipline is about training yourself to do what needs to be done whether you feel like doing it or not. (This has to be learned, we're not born with it.). To use spelling for this, suggest they take responsibility for sitting for five minutes (timed) and writing the words out *every day after school*, not all of them all at once or in two go's at the weekend! The target is self discipline, the evidence will be that they sat each day and wrote the words out for 5 minutes. They are simply using the words (which will be learned in the process) to help them develop self discipline. Again, the target is developing self discipline. Help them with the sentences.

Week 3: This week you might **focus on improving presentation skills** using spelling. To do this, examine the letters of each word (which will get learned in the process) and how to write them with the correct formation of the letters and the correct joins. Demonstrate how to do this with each word. Focus on the writing. When you look at their work, look at the writing and don't comment on the content, unless there is a glaring error.

Week 4: This week focus on **developing versatility.** To do this, suggest that every sentence they write must be about bananas. They love this!! Brainstorm and record first. Then write. Any list of words can be used in this way e.g.

- frog - dog - slog - fog

- The frog ate a banana and burped.

- The dog slipped on a banana and ran away shocked.

- Writing spelling sentences can be a slog, like picking bananas….

You get the idea!

Week 5: Using spelling words to **develop faster dictionary skills.** To do this, tell your child to find the words in the dictionary (did you know that if you just pick up and open a dictionary in the middle you will be near the m's? they might find that little tip helpful). Help them speed up their ability to find words in the dictionary by reminding them about alphabetical order and how the dictionary works. Better still, lay the alphabet out on the work space using plastic letters from the homework kit so that it is a bright, visual reference for the brain while they are using the dictionary.

Week 6: this week focus on **developing creativity** and putting ideas together. Choose a theme and when each word is put into a sentence, try to connect them to make a short story. Make helpful suggestions so that this becomes a brainstorming session, too. While your child is thinking, you can be writing it down for them to copy later. It is the head work that matters when you are developing creativity, not the writing it down which you can focus on another time.

Week 7: focus on **speeding up** while working carefully. After the sentence brainstorming, tell your child they're going to time how long it takes them to do one sentence. Write down the time and then discuss with them what they can do in themselves or around themselves to work a little faster. This is fun as long as there is no pressure. It needs to be done in the spirit of adventure, learning about themselves and their capabilities.

Week 8: focus on **reinforcing concentration.** Talk to your child about the need to be able to focus sometimes even when there are things around us to distract us. It's to do with self control which is not an easy thing to master. To help them develop their concentration and to reinforce it, put the tv on quietly for five minutes (timed) while they work on their words. Their job is to use their energy to focus on the spelling words and resist the tv! This will be a challenge for them! Remind them of the brain lesson and why they are getting distracted. Ask them to let you know if they really can't concentrate with it on (because they haven't developed that skill yet) and switch off, but say you will try again another time - and do it!

Week 9: focus on **communication skills.** Put the words on cards on the fridge and encourage the use of those words in conversations during the week. Include the whole family and make a little chart of who uses the words most. Parents, neighbours, carers - anyone who visits! Put a penny in a pot for every successful use and go and get a treat to reward the brain at the end of the week. With inflation, maybe slightly more than a penny?!

Week 10: focus on **preparation and/or organisation.** Tell your child that this week, they are going to work at getting everything ready themselves and have a 2 minute 'think' to see what help they need. Be nearby while this happens. You are asking them to review in themselves what they have achieved and what they are confident with in themselves. They need to reflect on this. Ask them what help they think they need for this week. Can they prepare by themselves? Do they need your help with organisation or can they now manage it on their own?

If you are focusing on ONE THING and you are presented with work that is below standard then you give your child that feedback and set a target for improving 'the thing that would make it better', another time.

Decide in advance what your child is going to do with the time if no homework is sent from school for the planned time. Brains like consistency. They also like to know in advance what to expect. Will it be free time? Or will your child use the time to practise reading skills or other skills that they are refining and developing instead? This way, their brain knows that that period of time is a 'work towards the future' development session. In which case, it still needs to have a target and to be timed.

Independently, or, if they are older, in discussion with your child, decide whether the session could be used for a review of what they have been doing and you can give them feedback on their successes and achievements since the beginning of term. Make it nice with a drink and snack and 'have a chat' with the aim of confirming and inspiring them. Alternatively, use the time to discuss new targets for the next few weeks. What can they focus on next to develop further?

It's a good opportunity to play skill enhancing games, too, such as memory games, or dice games to improve mental maths.

133

As soon as you decide to do something, the brain expects and organises itself to help you. As part of its job, it manufactures the energy needed to do it as well. If you then don't do whatever it was that was planned, there is excess energy in the system which needs to be deliberately re-focussed into a different activity or it will turn negative and create irritability or anger.

> When the parents returned from their extended holiday, they reported that their 9 year old daughter had, at first, been brilliant at doing all her set homework during the break; she had taken responsibility for working to the pre-prepared plan; read for 15 minutes each day; improved her organisation and cleared up after herself without needing to be told but then after four weeks she began to get difficult 'again'. What changed? The parents had been so delighted with her willingness, her achievement, her positive attitude and the prompt way she was doing it all, they got ambitious and decided to add more work to it, thereby breaking the agreement. Brains are very acute and if you agree something with your child, their brain will keep it and hold you to what you say. If you say 10 minutes, you must time 10 minutes and stop in 10 minutes or you will be in trouble! The child was to be confirmed and congratulated on her success; her positive attitude and her independence and supported in her objection to having the agreement broken *otherwise her brain would not make agreements in the same way again and* she would develop resentment instead.

Homework Kit Checklist

It's surprising how many tools may be needed to complete homework while children are at primary school. To avoid delays and time wasting, which can affect motivation and attitude, there is a checklist for parents who want to assemble a homework kit on the next page. It can make life so much easier if the equipment is stored in a specific place and checked on a regular basis to make sure it is ready for use when needed. It could be one of your child's responsibilities to go through the kit and check it at a scheduled time each week. It will help to point out they are building responsibility doing that.

Homework Kit Checklist

- Pen
- Pencils
- Colouring pencils
- Eraser
- Pencil sharpener
- Rulers - short and long
- Dictionary
- Thesaurus
- Protractor
- Compasses
- Glue stick

- Scissors
- Post-its of various colours
- Spare book marks
- Spelling practice sheets
- Rainbow tables*
- Timers - 1 / 5 / 20 / 30 minutes recommended
- Coins
- Dice
- Counters
- Paper
- Tracing paper
- First News - award winning children's newspaper (optional)
- String
- Elastic bands
- Hole punch
- Paper clips
- Plastic pockets for work

- Playing cards

- Plastic letters of the alphabet

- Stress ball

- Juggling balls

- Craft materials

- Background calming music (optional - it can give the brain continuity)

Cooling down your brain!

The environment is full of stimuli and trying to process it all can make brains 'speed up'. Here are some signs that your child's brain could be running too fast and needs slowing down:

- Over excited behaviour

- Not listening

- Loud

- Can't sleep

- Can't concentrate

- Unusually defiant

- Cheeky

- Reluctant to read aloud

Here are some activities which help to slow the brain down:

- Slow motion follow-the-leader (you lead, walking round the room)

- Juggling

- Colouring (there are lots of great colouring books available - keep one ready with a pack of colouring pencils for all members of the family to use)

- Tracing

- Count slowly in two's backwards and forwards until balance is restored :

    2…4…6…8…6…4…2…4…6…8…6…4…2…4…6…

. It will help your child if you explain to them how their behaviour is affected when their brain is rushing. If they can understand 'what is happening to them' when they can't sleep or have had too much technology or sugar for example and you give them ways to manage it, they will know what to do to help themselves when they need to calm or slow down.

Lesson 15:
A Way to Think about Skills, Children and Development

Being able to boil an egg does not mean you can produce a gourmet meal! Likewise, being able to 'sit up straight and fold your arms', does not mean you are able to listen! Each skill - gourmet cooking and listening - is a complex series of actions which need to be coordinated for a person to accomplish them. For that reason, they would be described here as 'Master Skills' which are the result of developing many little skills, called here 'Mini Skills'.

Below is a list of 'Master Skills' your child needs to develop during their primary years. These are the skills that become part of your child's core foundation throughout life. It is not exhaustive. You are encouraged to add your own examples to this in the pages for your notes at the end of this book. Brainstorm with your partner, fellow parents, friends and teachers **how you can use homework** (and everyday life) to help *your* child develop them. They are all broken down into the 'Mini Skills' that you need to be able to do to accomplish the Master Skill. Whenever you spot your child doing or practising one of the 'Mini Skills', such as stopping when asked (demonstrating self control), confirm that they are on the right track by pointing it out and saying 'well done, you stopped yourself when I asked you and that showed great self control,' then *their brain will know* what that mini skill is called and what they need to practise.

Here are some examples of Master and the Mini Skills needed to achieve them:

Master skill: Listening

Mini skills leading to success with the master skill of Listening:

- able to stop what they are doing

- able to focus and make eye contact
- able to concentrate
- able to wait
- able to make connection with reference
- able to reflect
- able to sort
- able to take in information
- able to respond appropriately

Master skill: Thinking

Mini skills leading to success with the master skill of Thinking:

- able to gather reference
- able to make connections
- able to sort
- able to analyse
- able to prioritise
- able to categorise
- able to sequence

- able to be systematic
- able to reason
- able to deduce
- able to focus;
- able to concentrate
- able to estimate
- able to rationalise

Master skill: Comprehension

Mini skills leading to achievement of comprehension:

- able to decode
- able to focus
- able to read
- able to evaluate
- able to interpret
- able to reference
- able to make connections
- able to deduce

- able to follow a story

- able to predict

- able to infer

- able to be systematic

By breaking down the Master Skills this way, we can identify where a child needs to focus to progress and achieve. However, these are not exhaustive lists. Your child is a complex, processing being with the urge to develop and grow. They will do that at their own pace and according to the input, opportunities and experiences they are given.

Here are more **Master Skills** for you to brainstorm and break down into mini skills that you can work on with your child; a few examples are given for each one, but space is left for you to think about your own child and set specific targets for - and with - them. The question you need to ask to identify what is needed is: What does my child need to be able to do so that they can learn to…… (insert Master Skill)?

Example:

What does my child need to be able to concentrate?

Is it:

- Better listening skills?

- Better comprehension - they can't understand the instruction and get bored?

- Help to manage anxiety or other feelings?

- Help to manage distractions?

- More sleep?

- An understanding of expectations?

- Help to take responsibility?

- The definition of what concentration means?

- A change in the environment?

- Less pressure?.....

There can be many reasons for a child's lack of concentration (or achievement of a Master Skill) and each child is unique. By giving some thought to what *your* child needs help with so that they can achieve one of the Master Skills, you will be able to set targets for each of the mini-skills. Master Skills take time, work and effort to develop but by thinking about them in this way, you can create a 'development plan' for each of them. Your child will love being given little steps that they can do and that are achievable. Use homework sessions to help them achieve those. You will find out what they need in any area by observation; by reflecting on the experiences they have had in life; by talking to them - one boy couldn't concentrate because his classroom was too stuffy and he didn't know what to do about it - and/or by talking to their teacher about how they are at school.

As you work through the following Master Skills (M.S.) to uncover the areas your child needs to focus on; bear in mind, there will be overlaps. For example, you need to be able to focus to achieve any of the Master Skills. They are not in any specific order.

M. S. Communication

- be able to express themselves

- to listen

- to empathise

M. S. Organisation

- know where things go

- be able to sort

- be able to classify

M. S. Self management and self discipline

- be able to wait

- don't interrupt

- be able to follow instructions

M. S. Brain training - includes: Memory/problem solving/thinking

- ask appropriate questions

- can sequence

- can memorise (the different ways to memorise can be broken down too!)

M. S. Concentration

M. S. Presentation (how the world sees you and how you see yourself)

M. S. Fine motor (cutting, gripping, manipulating) and **Gross motor** (sports)

For a child to achieve competence in a skill there is **a lot of work** that needs to go into helping them.

- they need the definition of that skill;

- they need to know what behaviour goes with it (so they can recognise it in themselves and others);

- they need to know what it feels like when they do it right;

- they need to know what it feels like when they don't do it right;

- they need to know the vocabulary that goes with the skill and

- they need to know exactly what they are doing to be in control of the skill

Next time you are with a young child and you wonder why they're not listening, look to see what mini skill they need to work on to improve their overall listening skill and guide them with that.

Poem:
The culture that we live in

The culture that we live in
Makes living very fast
It goes against our nature
Our lives are whizzing past

So much presents itself to us
Each moment of the day
There's little time to think, reflect,
There's stress in every day

For children it is just the same
It's puzzling to be here
Born equipped with all the tools
They find there's much to fear

To lose fine sensitivities
To stop exploring - fast
Don't question, just do what you're told
But soon your life is past

The children feel most all they meet
And most of it's not seen
To judge their feelings while they grow
Just makes them feel unclean

This feeling then takes all their glow
The start to dim and hide
For feelings they're afraid to show
And questions stay inside

So nurturing the best in them
Is simple for to do
Let them respond with what they have
The onus is on you

Please be perceptive, grow yourself
Be watchful with more care
You're dealing with a human being
And they're becoming rare.

100 things to learn before you're 10

Lesson 16:
What children need to know about habits

> A bright, creative 12 year old boy was underperforming, underachieving and constantly getting into trouble at school. At home, too, he was only wanting to play for hours on his X-box. But then he realised that it was an important year for him because at the end of it, he would be sitting exams that would determine which school he would attend next. His parents were very concerned and so were his teachers. Change was needed and quickly. A little while after his realisation, the boy seemed to be making positive progress and then unfortunately, he got into trouble at school. This was a great disappointment, to him and to his family. He said he had been making an effort but that he'd been in the 'wrong place at the wrong time' and the teacher thought he had instigated the trouble. He had tried to explain this at the time, but was given detention for his 'attitude'.

A situation like this will undermine progress and can make a child feel their efforts count for nothing, that there is no point in even trying because there is nothing acknowledging their effort or the progress they are making. When this happens - or preferably, *before* anything like this happens - one thing that can prevent a return to negative behaviour is to give your child an explanation about habits; how they develop, how they work and why we need to be careful about the habits we grow. To do this, it helps the brain if you draw a picture as you talk to your child as follows:

Imagine this is a field full of grass....

Draw a field full of grass

100 things to learn before you're 10

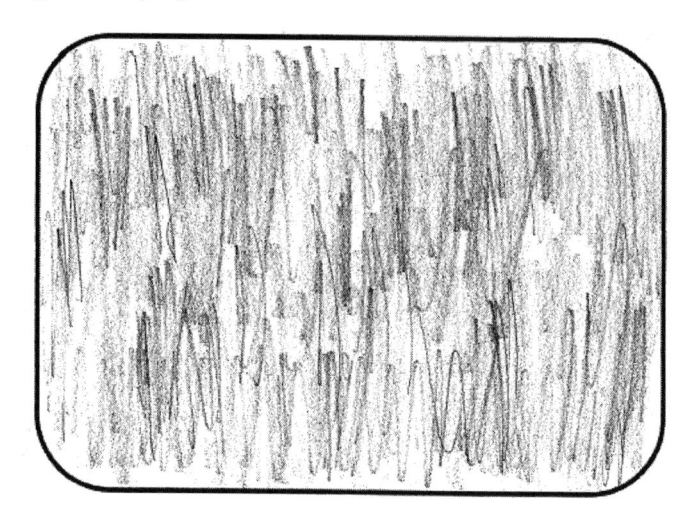

And suppose there is a gate on one side here *(A)* and another on the other side of the field over here *(B)*

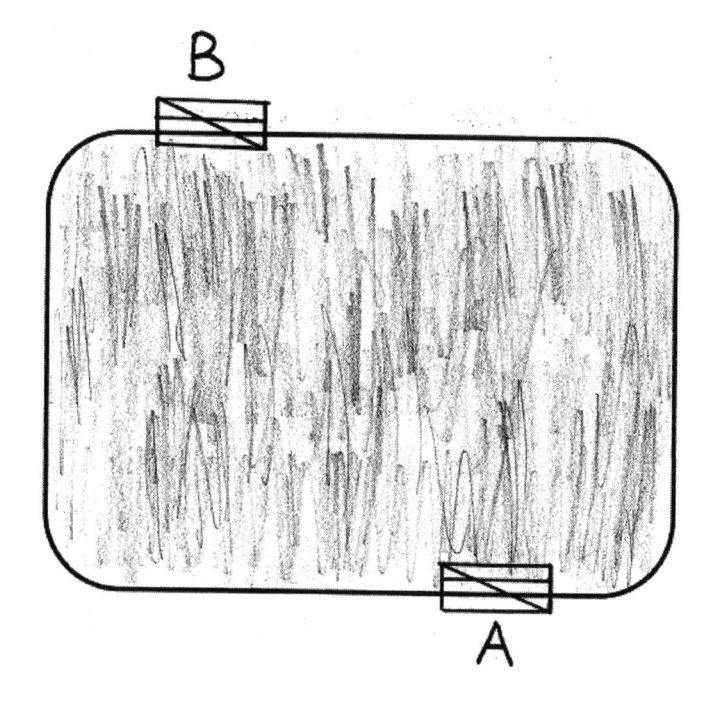

100 things to learn before you're 10

Now suppose, one day, I walk from Gate A, across the field to Gate B. If you were watching, you would see that I would make a faint path by walking through the long grass.

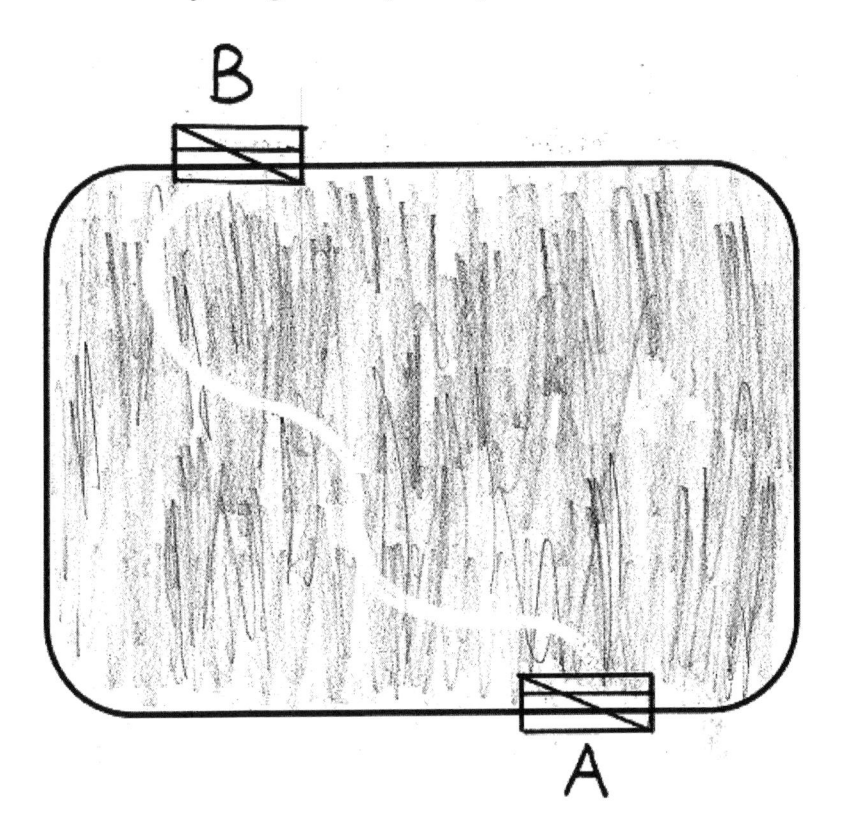

Add to your diagram with a faint line from A to B

If I do that just once, after a little while, the grass would spring back to normal and you wouldn't be able to see that I had walked across the field. If I walk from A to B just a few times, it would be the same; the grass would soon spring back to where it was and you wouldn't be able to see which way I had walked.

100 things to learn before you're 10

BUT, suppose I walk across that field on the same path every day for a year. The grass would have been trampled down and broken so much that everyone would be able to see the path I had walked.

Diagram as above with a very thick line from A to B

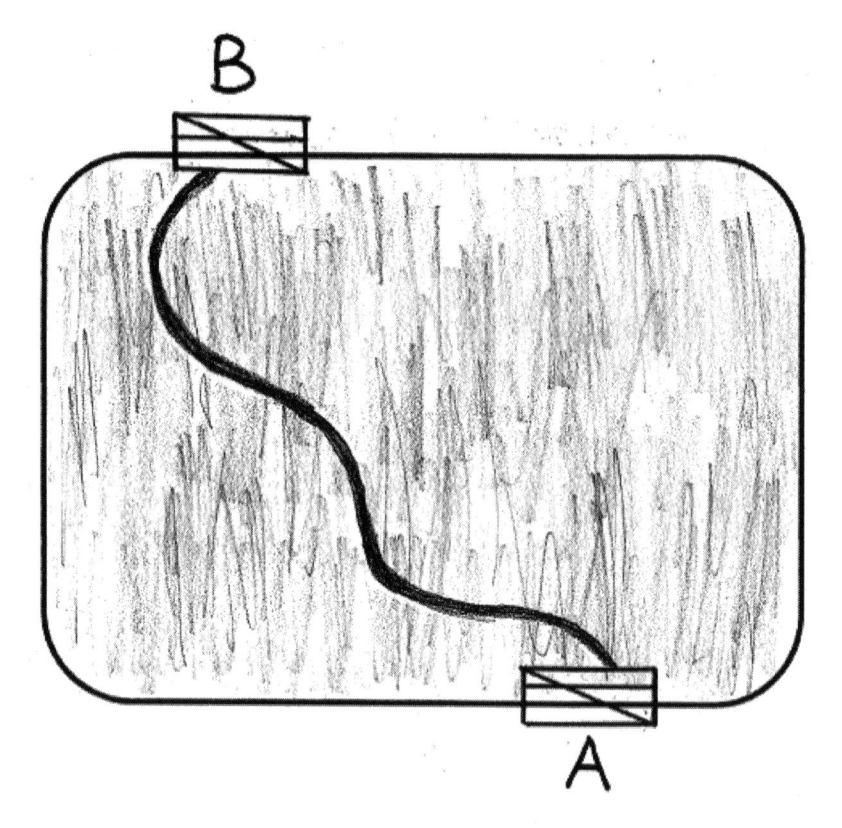

This is what habits are like. If we do something once or twice or even three times, nothing much will happen, no one will know. BUT, if we do that behaviour over and over again, our brain programs it to become automatic so that we don't need to think about it any more. That's great, *if that's what we want.*

100 things to learn before you're 10

However, suppose we place a raging bull on one side of the field and we've been told that if we walk on that path, the bull will harm us! We need to make a different path across the field. That's what it's like trying to make a different, brand new habit, because the first one is getting us into trouble. At first it can feel difficult, because we have to find the right way; then we have to push through the thick grass again, which means we have to think about what we are doing. It is not as easy as the well worn path. We can sometimes get tired of making the new path and suddenly find ourselves back on the first one because it is automatic and will feel as though it is pulling us back! That's ok as long as we notice and get back to making the new one, which we know will be better for us because the bull can't get us there.

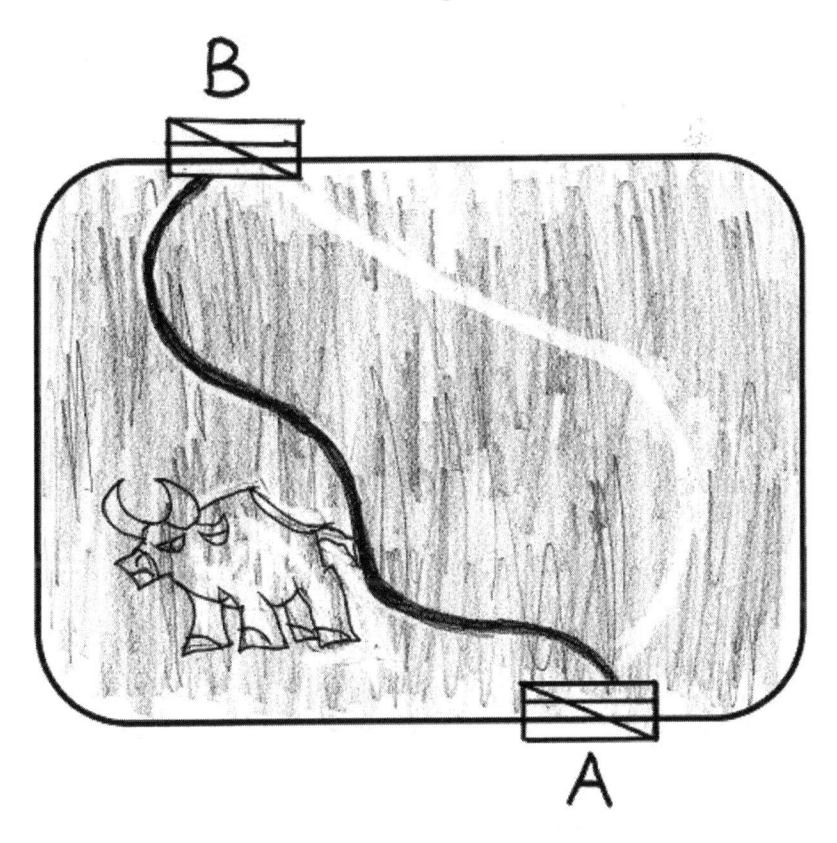

The trouble is, you are not the only one who develops habits! You can be making your new path, but until you have done it long enough, when people look in the field, they will expect to see you on the old path. They have habits too and are used to seeing you behave the 'old' way, so although you know you are on a different path, they don't see you there because they are looking through their habit! After a while - about 3-4 weeks - as long as you keep going on the new path, developing the new behaviour, your teachers will start to think there's something 'different' about you; they will start to notice your improved behaviour and they will start to congratulate and praise you for it. Then you will know you have succeeded. The old path will grow over and disappear with time and the new one will become automatic because your brain will see that you keep repeating that behaviour so you must want it as your new development.

Important note: it is much easier to change a habit when you are young than later. This is because the foundation you are building as a child, does not 'set' until later on. Once it is crystallised (set), when you become an adult, it is much harder - and takes longer - to change.

Talking to your child in this way allows them to be conscious of the processes that are going on in them. By sharing this reference with them, you can give them reflection on their behaviour at any time, pointing out, 'is that a useful habit to grow in your life?' or 'what are you trying to achieve with that behaviour?'. It will help you guide them towards developing the best of themselves and managing their own behaviour.

For further information about habits, Charles Duhigg's book: The Power of Habit is an excellent, recommended resource.

Poem: Habit

If parents wouldn't listen
The boy would find a way
To get their full attention
Any time of night or day

When first he started out to swear
They thought it was amusing
They'd laugh at this young toddler
Who found it quite confirming

And then as he got older
Frustration grew as well
He started hitting, kicking too
His parents' smiles fell

Trouble followed quickly
The parents were afraid
They saw the harm that had been done
But could it be unmade?

It could take years to undo this
To change the boy's behaviour
Knowing it, you're halfway there
Realisation is the saviour

So, habits, absolutely yes,
Take care with what you learn
Program to help the best of you
Success is what you'll earn

100 things to learn before you're 10

50 Most Loved, Most Used, Most Useful Books for Children from 4 -12 years old selected from the Teacher's Personal Collection….

Each of these books have been used time and time again to:

- engage reluctant readers

- ignite a passion for reading (all the way up to 12 years old)

- teach concept of number

- teach creative writing, framework or structure

- inspire young artists to experiment with different drawing/illustrating styles

- trigger discussion (including sensitive issues, such as bereavement*)

- teach punctuation

- teach listening skills

- improve expression in reading

- teach presentation skills

- improve reading aloud

- examine humour

- improve observation skills

100 things to learn before you're 10

- enjoy and appreciate rhythm and rhyme

- improve comprehension (including preparation for 7+ 8+ 11+ exams) and more

All and any of these books have been useful for teaching one or more aspects listed above. However, they have been arranged into 'Start with these' categories to get you going… but don't limit yourself or your child's experience by only looking at *those* books for help in *that* category. All the books listed are great for teaching in a variety of ways. This selection would make an excellent first 'Children's Library', for all your children.

Start with these to read with and to children who lack confidence or who need switching on to reading (including those with learning differences)

Don't Let the Pigeon Drive the Bus	Mo Willems
Watch Me Throw the Ball	Mo Willems
There is a Bird on Your Head	Mo Willems
Little Beauty	Anthony Brown
Slow Loris	Alexis Deacon
Beware of the Frog	William Bee
The Book with No Pictures	B. J. Novak
That is NOT a Good Idea	Mo Willems
Meerkat Mail	Emily Gravett
Spells	Emily Gravett

These are particularly useful for developing observation and memory skills:

Puzzle Island	Paul Adshead - 8+
Enigma	Graeme Base - 8+
Can You See Sassoon	Sam Usher - 4+
Find Chaffy	Jamie Smart - 7+
Who's Hiding	Satoru Onishi - 7+
Lookalikes	Joan Steiner - 7+

100 things to learn before you're 10

Start with these for anything related to maths and number:

How Much is a Million	David M Schwartz
365 Penguins	Jean-Luc Fromental
Just a Second	Steve Jenkins
One Grain of Rice	Demi
How Big is a Million	Anna Milbourne
Sir Cumference and the first Round Table	Cindy Neuschwander

Fabulous for rhythm and rhyme:

Superworm	Julia Donaldson
Perky Little Penguins	Tony Mitton
Hubble Bubble Granny Trouble	Tracey Corderoy
Freddie and the Fairy	Julia Donaldson
Bubble Trouble	Margaret Mahy
You Can't Take an Elephant on the Bus	Patricia Cleveland-Peck
Iggy Peck Architect	Andrea Beaty
Have You Seen Who's Just Moved In Next Door to Us?	Colin McNaughton
A Squash and a Squeeze	Julia Donaldson
I don't Want a Posh Dog	Emma Dodd

These are great inspiration for children who love art and creativity:

Zoom	Istvan Banyai
AGAIN!	Emily Gravett
The Paradise Garden	Colin Thompson
The Paperbag Prince	Colin Thompson
Castles	Colin Thompson
Pictures of Home	Colin Thompson
Puss Jekyll Cat Hyde	Joyce Dunbar

100 things to learn before you're 10

Start with these for discussion or for working on comprehension:

Flotsam	David Weisner
The Giving Tree	Shel Silverstein
The Arrival	Shaun Tan
The Secret Lives of Princesses	Philippe Lechermeier
Hello, Mr. Hulot	David Merveille/Jacques Tati
The Day I Swapped My Dad for Two Goldfish	Neil Gaiman
The Conductor	Laetitia Deverna

Most helpful book for managing anxiety:

Silly Billy — Anthony Browne

Helpful books for talking about loss and bereavement:

Duck, Death and the Tulip*	Wolf Erlbruch
No Matter What*	Debi Gliori
Up in Heaven*	Emma Chichester-Clark

100 things to learn before you're 10

Top 21 Most Loved and used Games and Activities for Teaching Skills to primary aged children

Skills take time to develop. They need practise. Your child needs to build the neural pathways that anchor the skill in their brain. This means repetition. The conscious brain will get bored with the repetition so you need to find ways to engage it. Games are a brilliant tool for doing this. They can provide the motivation and the repetition to practise the skills. The following games are well loved by children and a lot of fun for everyone! You don't always need to 'play the game' as it is written, but be creative with the resource and adapt it to create the experience that will support your target. Always identify the skills your child is developing while they are playing and confirm how well that skill is developing as they get better at it.

Each game or activity will help with more than one skill, but focus only on one at a time each time you do the activity. All activities and games can be adapted for use with all ages from 5-11 years, depending on how you use them and what you are helping your child to develop. Explain the reason for the activity or game before your child starts it so their brain assimilates and anchors it.

ACTIVITIES: no or low cost resources

TRACING use to develop the following in all ages up to 10 years:

- pencil control - choose increasingly difficult pictures to trace (this is an effective way to start the process of changing a habit of poor handwriting)

- concentration - don't take the pencil off until you have completed the whole item - be aware of what is happening in you

- care - stay exactly on the line all the way round

JUGGLING can be a way to:

- stimulate the brain

- get quick success for a child with low self esteem providing you help and guide (learning to throw and catch)

- develop persistence

- improve hand/eye coordination

- develop focus and concentration

- learn to unwind/relax

JIGSAW PUZZLES

- matching shape

- holding 'the bigger picture'

- encourage the brain to mentally project/imagine

- learn to sort and categorise

- teach organisation skills

SPOT THE DIFFERENCE

- learn and practise being systematic

- improve observation skills

- practise memory skills
- focus and concentration

GAMES that can be purchased.

It is worthwhile investing in games that are versatile and can support your child's development. Remember to let your child know what they are focusing on and **why** they are doing this game or the activity! Invest in games that are versatile! The following purchased games have been useful for a variety of reasons, as shown.

BLINK

- Use the cards to teach and practise sorting
- Play the game to increase the brain's processing speed
- Use the cards to teach addition to 5yrs.
- Use the cards to teach simple subtraction

SUPER CIRCLES - card game

- This is a more advanced sorting game for improving processing speed

DOBBLE - card game

- Use to improve observation skills
- Use to teach and practise organisation skills

- Play the game(s) to increase processing speed

PAIRS - the card game

- use to teach and practise memory skills
- use to teach and practise organisation skills
- identification

DISTRACTION

- improve number bonds
- improve mental maths
- improve memory
- stimulate creativity by answering the questions

CATCH the MATCH

- improve observation
- organisation
- develop systematic approach

CAMOUFLAGE

- develop strategic thinking

- be systematic
- organisation
- interpretation
- meet criteria
- develop reasoning

SET

- organisation skills
- ordering
- sorting
- making comparisons
- reasoning

CHOCOLATE FIX

- develop and practise reasoning
- develop logical thinking
- follow instructions
- systematic

similar to Camouflage

HUE KNEW

- speed of process

- speed of reflexes

- mental maths (adding up own score)

KNOT-SO-FAST

- interpret diagrams

- hold information in the brain (helps working memory)

- translate picture to reality

MAKE'N'BREAK

- hold an image in mind

- practise visualisation

- speed and accuracy

- timing and activity

LOOK! LOOK!

- Improves observation and identification

MATCHING MADNESS – Ravensburger

- useful for increasing working memory

COLOUR CODE

- helpful for teaching sequencing
- improves visualisation

NUBBLE

- excellent for mental maths practise
- prime numbers
- addition, subtraction, multiplication, division
- strategic thinking

A note about technology:

There are many apps and programs which claim to help your child develop skills. These can be very helpful for repetition, if the child is motivated. However, it is wise to exercise caution with technology while the brain is developing. In world history terms, technology is in its infancy and we simply do not know its long term effects on the developing brain, whether positive or negative. One thing is certain, there is absolutely nothing that beats human interaction and its essential feedback from someone they trust - be it a parent, teacher, grandparent, aunt, uncle etc. - when your child is developing their matrix of connections. The foundation built in our pre-puberty years, is our foundation for life. It cannot be changed. It can only be managed after it has crystallised during adolescence.

Read more about the effects of technology on the developing brain in Reset Your Child's Brain by Victoria Dunckley.

100 things to learn before you're 10

Whatever any child is doing, *something* will be developing in their foundation. The question that needs to be asked is: What are they *actually* learning from what they are now doing? Although there are many things to learn before you're ten, The 100 Things to Learn that follow are the ones that have been most needed to engage and motivate children. It is not an exhaustive list and space has been left for your own notes.

Some core messages have been included for speed of reference. They are not the *only* messages that children need to know, but they are sometimes overlooked or forgotten messages...

1. **Attitude** - this can be changed. To change a negative attitude to a positive your child needs help to go deeper in their thinking to get to a place of reason. The Two Lives and The Brain help when you are trying to help your child change a negative attitude to a positive one.

2. **Awareness** - awareness of who and what they are can secure the growth mindset your child was born with and help to prevent the depreciation of it by negative experience. The Two Lives helps with this.

3. **Action -** actions that are repeated over and over again are an instruction to the brain. It makes automatic the things that are done repeatedly. Children need to know this.

4. **Addition -** this is an essential part of maths, which trains your brain to think in different ways. Adding is the easiest mathematical process to observe.

5. **Anger -** is a powerful surge of energy intended to correct things which have gone wrong. It is not always used wisely and can damage us and others by using a huge amount of emotional energy very quickly. Children need to know that it is part of their job to learn to manage their feelings and not

always react to them without thinking. It takes practise to manage anger.

6. **Adolescence** - the time in our life when the foundation we have built starts to get organised and crystallises.

7. **Behaviour** - It helps children to know that part of their job of a child is to learn to control and manage their behaviour. This takes practise.

8. **Boundaries** - while you learn to control and manage yourself, boundaries keep you safe and make you feel secure because what you can and cannot do are made very clear to your brain.

9. **Balance** - too much of anything can affect how we feel and make us less effective in what we do. Our feelings tell us when we are out of balance. It is important to listen to their guidance.

10. **Brain** - your brain is meant to work for you not the other way round!

11. **Best** - children need to be shown what their best looks like. 'Best behaviour' can be commented on, 'best work' needs to be demonstrated. If it is possible for a human to do it, it is possible for you!

12. **Confidence** - we get confidence from 'doing'. If you don't know how to do, ask someone to teach you.

13. **Concentration** - this is a skill. You can improve it. The Brain Lesson will help.

14. **Care** - we build only one foundation for life. Work carefully to keep development options open as long as you can.

15. **Communication** - one of the reasons we learn languages. Avoid assumption for effective communication.

16. **Creativity** - this is part of your core to grow and develop. It makes you different…you are not meant to be the same as everyone else!

17. **Choice** - parents are there to help you make choices while you learn about the world and develop the ability to make positive choices for yourself.

18. **Consequences** - we cause consequences by what we do. There can be good and bad consequences!

19. **Comprehension** - means using our brain to connect new information with what we already know and figuring out something else as a result

20. **Change** - an essential part of the life process but the World Life changes in unpredictable ways, the Natural Life is more reliable and predictable.

21. **Danger** - Children need to understand the dangers of development such as unhelpful habits, negative attitudes, mindset and behaviours, as well as the dangers of the world we are in, if they are to protect and manage themselves effectively.

22. **Development** - the core purpose of human life. What you develop matters, because you add it to the world and it can be positive or negative.

23. **Direction** - what are you aiming at? what do you need to learn to achieve it? Knowing this helps to occupy your brain purposefully.

24. **Division** - this is a manmade phenomenon. Nature adds, takes away and multiplies, but doesn't divide. Children find this the hardest maths concept to grasp. (for the scientists among you, cells don't actually divide, they multiply!)

25. **Decision making** - something that you learn to do and get better at with experience. You need to know what you want and what is good for you and not good for you.

26. **Effort** - is what we use to learn new things - it is often part of the learning process and a sign that progress may be made

27. **Energy** - everything we do uses energy! Some things use more energy than others.

28. **Experience** - part of what we gather and grow as we go through life. We can use it to get better at achieving our goals and to help other people.

29. **Effect** - what we do has an effect in us and outside us.

30. **Expectations** - children need to be told and need to understand what is expected of them as well as what they can expect from others.

31. **Emotions** - part of what we need to experience life. Feelings are a guide. They are not always accurate.

32. **Focus** - focus is something we learn to control. Being mesmerised by a screen is not focus.

33. **Fear** - something that alerts us to the need for caution or change.

34. **Foundation** - what you build in yourself during childhood. It is made from knowledge, habits, attitudes and mindset. It affects your whole life one way or another.

35. **Future** - if you want to be hardworking in your future, start now.

36. **Formulas -** the formula for your success will depend on what you want to achieve, how thorough you are and how hard you work for it.

37. **Generation -** the moment we agree to do something, our brain generates the energy for us to do it. If we don't follow through with the action, that energy turns negative and can make us irritable. The energy created has to be used somehow! Be careful what you generate. The culture encourages us to intend too much!

38. **Gratitude -** it's important to feel gratitude. It encourages humility.

39. **Generosity -** when you are generous; others are generous with you; this generates more positive energy into the world.

40. **Handwriting -** children need to know they can influence how people think about them by what they do and this can attract positive energy to them (praise) or negative (criticism). Being praised feels better than being criticised so presentation skills are important.

41. **How we work -** we work best according to the laws of nature

42. **Homework -** use this to train your brain, practise skills, gather reference and develop independence and self discipline.

43. **Habits -** these are automatic patterns of behaviour that can be helpful or not very helpful. Anything, good or bad, that we do over and over can becomes a habit.

44. **Inspiration -** an important thing to be and to have.

45. **Initiative -** taking the initiative means you think for yourself and have the courage to act on what you believe is right.

46. **Independence** - is earned by taking and demonstrating responsibility.

47. **Imagination** - a tool for every human being to use to make the world a better place

48. **Joy** - the feeling we get from a job well done

49. **Judgement** - something we need to use carefully

50. **Juggling** - a brilliant brain training tool

51. **Knowledge** - your brain needs as much knowledge and reference as possible to be able to create new things

52. **Kindness** - this is an important human quality to value and grow.

53. **Laws** - there are two kinds: natural and manmade. Work as closely as possible with the natural laws and protect yourself in the culture with the manmade ones! *How* we grow and develop is pre-set, *what* we grow and develop is our choice.

54. **Language** - a tool of communication. The better your child's reference and vocabulary, the better they can express themselves and understand others.

55. **Loss** - we cannot win at everything in life. What can you learn all the times that you don't?

56. **Listening** - this is something we DO. It is not something that 'happens'. It is an important communication skill and development tool

57. **Money** - a World Life resource. Keep a bowl of small change available for counting, sorting and money questions. Children no longer shop like they used to do and need practise to feel confident with money problem solving at school.

58. **Memory** - there are at least six ways to help our brains remember things; by sight, by sound, by touch, smell, taste or a mixture of these. Use this information to help in your learning.

59. **Measurement** - only possible in a physical body.

60. **Mistakes** - we are meant to make them, refine and move on.

61. **Multiplication** - learning tables is easy; it takes 3 minutes a day and no stress. See the example is in the Brain Lesson section.

62. **Nervous** - when a lot of people get anxious about something, like exams, the energy generated can be a nervous energy. If we get involved with it, we can think we are nervous, too, which sends emotional energy into the brain and stops it working so efficiently! To clear your head, take three deep breaths so your brain gets oxygen; calm yourself by breathing slowly and walking slowly for 20 steps. Understanding The Brain Lesson really well can help with revision and exams.

63. **Naughty** - not a very helpful word because it doesn't suggest improvement.

64. **Noise** - can interrupt thinking processes and cause dispersion and frustration. To work properly, we all need quiet at times and to respect others by not interrupting them when they are thinking.

65. **Observation** - study everything that lives. It all has an affect on our world and on each of us. It is important reference. Watch to find out how things work.

66. **Organisation** - essential for health and the prevention of overwhelm, which is common in the culture of today

67. **Ordering** - essential for efficiency

68. **Purpose** - stay with your natural purpose of personal development. Getting sidetracked can lead to dissatisfaction at core.

69. **Problem solving** - what brains are for

70. **Priority** - Natural Life first. Core first.

71. **Planning** - essential for health and well being. What do YOU need?

72. **Presentation** - it matters because of what you cause and what you attract

73. **Potential** - the difference between you and your potential, is work. Children need to know this!

74. **Questions** - never stop asking - especially 'why?' and 'how'.

75. **Quiet** - rests our systems so we can cool down and reset/refresh them. It is an important part of self respect that we sometimes stay quiet to let ourselves and others repair or think.

76. **Respect** - this is important for our self worth and to show value for other people

77. **Rest** - this is just as important as work, our health depends on it

78. **Responsibility** - a necessary part of independence

79. **Reference** - your brain is hungry for as much reference as possible

80. **Ruler** - learn to use a ruler carefully as part of developing fine motor skills

81. **Systems** - this is to do with the way we do things. Try to create systems that will support you, like nature does

82. **Success** - is making a decision and following through

83. **Subtraction** - taking away - children recognise it as part of a natural process

84. **Sharing** - an important part of being human

85. **Senses** - one of our main tools for development guidance - to get a full picture about something, we can use all our senses on it

86. **Skills** - bring satisfaction, confidence and independence

87. **Self view** - love what and who you are without judgement

88. **Self belief** - you are a mix of talent, experience and intelligence; when you are doing what you were designed to do, do it with confidence

89. **Standards** - high standards take effort to establish and maintain, but bring security and pride. Know what you can rely on in yourself

90. **Targets** - always give your brain something to aim at so it keeps working for you

91. **Trust** - extremely valuable and rare in the world. It is a natural life quality to grow and develop. Treasure it and don't break it. When you lose trust in something, it is a life changing event. Children need to know this.

92. **Thinking skills** - brains work in different ways. Train your brain to develop logic, analysis, reasoning, sequencing and order. Thinking is our slowest process. It is a highly sophisticated process of putting new ideas or information with

things already in our brain so that it can create something new or solve a problem.

93. **Time** - one thing we cannot change; we need to learn to manage our expectations and the expectations everyone else has so that we use it wisely.

94. **Technology** - perceived as an essential 21st century tool. Be careful screens don't lure you away from your development path by fascinating your brain.

95. **Understanding** the difference between you and the culture helps to keep you on a development journey.

96. **Unique** - you are designed to be different, in every way you, your body, your brain and your experience are unique and can never be duplicated. Only you can do the job that you are designed to do.

97. **Value** - find out what is real and value it always - human qualities are one thing to value along with self respect and respect for others, especially those who support you.

98. **Vocabulary** - improve communication - work hard to grow your reference and improve your vocabulary. It helps confidence to grow.

99. **Vision** - bear in mind how you want to be and what you want to achieve so that you keep working towards it

100. **World** - there is only one you and only one World. The World loves your potential and supports you totally, physically, mentally, emotionally and spiritually, even if you don't care to think about it! Being the best you can be at any time, means you are a radiating a positive presence in the World which is a huge benefit for everyone. You already make a difference.